The Second Eve

Understanding Biblical Equality

The Second Eve

Understanding Biblical Equality

Bette J. Boersma

Foreword by Gladys Hunt

Christians for Biblical Equality
122 W Franklin Ave Ste 218
Minneapolis MN 55404-2451
Ph: 612-872-6898 Fax: 612-872-6891
Email: cbe@cbeinternational.org
Website: http://www.cbeinternational.org

Junia Publishing
Grandville, Michigan

The Second Eve

We would love to hear from you. Send comments, questions, book orders or contact the author with the information below.

Attention churches, small groups, Christian education departments, bookstores, etc. Quantity discounts available for bulk purchases of this book for group study, promotional premiums, gifts, fund raisers or resale.

Junia Publishing
PO Box 381
Jenison, MI 49429 0381

on the web: juniapublishing.com

e-mail the author: bette@juniapublishing.com

ISBN: 0-9770240-0-8
LCCN: 2005905295

Scripture references, unless otherwise noted, are from the King James Version. Other versions used include the New International Version (NIV, International Bible Society, 1973), The New King James Bible (NKJ, Thomas Nelson, 1982), the Revised Standard Version (RSV) and Today's New International Version (TNIV).
Cover Design by Eric Schafer
Cover Art by Elizabeth DeBraber, used by permission.
Article: "Crafting a Church without Walls" by Lola Scobey was first printed in the Fall 2002 issue of *Mutuality* (CBE International), used by permission.

Acknowledgments

I gratefully acknowledge the work and scholarship of Linda Belleville, Gilbert Bilezikian, Gordon D. Fee, Rebecca Merrill Groothuis, Mary Hayter, David F. Noble, Aida Basancon Spencer and William David Spencer for ideas and material in this study. (See the Works Cited page for a detailed list of sources.)

I personally owe a debt of gratitude to the following three churches because of their courage in confronting the issues of men and women in relationships and ministry: New Day Community Church in Kalamazoo, Michigan, Mars Hill Church and HomeFront Church in Grandville, Michigan.

Thanks also go to Liz DeBraber, not only for her embroidered painting *Justice*, featuring the Rev. Charlotte Ellison, which appears on the cover, but also for her artistic contribution to the issue of equality through her series of portraits called "Celebrating Women in Ministry."

I owe a debt of gratitude to Eric Schafer for his graphic design expertise as well as his encouragement and enthusiasm for this project. Also to members of the local chapter of CBE (Grand Rapids, Michigan) for their encouragement and support, and their lively discussions of each chapter during our monthly book study.

Preface

The Second Eve has in many ways been a joint effort between my husband of thirty-six years and myself. It began, admittedly, with my own challenge to traditional ways of thinking, but many of the ideas and discoveries that came into being during several years of searching, reading and discussing came about because of Hank's thoughts and challenges. This book is the culmination of a study that essentially changed both of our thinking about the issue of women's roles in both the church and the home.

Our desire is not to convince Christians to believe as we do, for we believe the task of leading us into all truth belongs to the Holy Spirit (John 16:13). Nor do we claim to have checked every source or to give the final word on this difficult subject. Rather, for the sake of all those who are seeking, we have attempted to summarize and explain the things we have learned and to set them down as clearly and understandably as we can. Our desire is for all who read The Second Eve to be blessed and learn something new about the heart of God toward women and their ministry.

Contents

Foreword by Gladys Hunt

"There are no ordinary human beings," wrote C. S. Lewis. "You have never talked to a mere mortal... It is immortals whom we joke with, work with, marry, snub and exploit." If these solemn words are true (and they are) we need to go to the Scriptures with fresh eyes and see where we have gone wrong in the way we treat each other.

The most astounding truth about who we are is found in the first chapter of Genesis. God creates the world by the Word of his power. Then he arranges its details and furnishes it, getting it ready for the crown of his creation: human beings in his own image. (Genesis 1: 26,27) Male and female in the image of God. Then he puts his newly created world in their charge. It's a joint venture for male and female.

God knows the joy of fellowship within the Godhead: three persons in one being. He speaks of himself in plural form when he says, "Let us make human beings in our image, in our likeness." In an expanded accounting of God's creative plan (Genesis 2), God gives the man the experience of aloneness so he will know how much he needs a counterpart. None of the creatures who appear before the man for a naming ceremony are remotely like him. He is alone! God made his first negative evaluation about his creation when he said, "It is not good for the man to be alone."

So God makes the woman (and the details of how this is done are significant) and brings her to the man. How perfect she must have been so fresh from the hand of God. The man cries with joy as he acknowledges the wisdom and grace of God, "This at last is bone of my bone and flesh of my flesh!"

God exists in community; he wants man to know the joy of community. Two people, alike and yet different, but both in the image of God. God decrees two people become one flesh in the marriage relationship. And since both male and female are made in his image, it seems likely that every other human endeavor would profit from the input of both male and female.

This is awesome! I am made in the image of God and so are you. An awareness of this will surely change how I live and relate to both God and other people. It also raises the question, How do I treat someone else made in the image of God?

Everyone needs to know who they are. And this is the place to begin: made in the image of God.

Over the centuries this seminal truth that it takes both male and female to reflect the image of God has become distorted both within society and in the church, where it should be most honored. As a result the church has often taught a doctrine of superiority of the male and has given women a lesser place. It's been a "he paints and she carries the pail" kind of world for many women, who struggle to know who they are and how to use their giftedness.

Women find good news when they study the Scriptures and find out that they, too, are made in the image of God, and have been given dominion over the world God has made. What does this mean? What about the Scriptures quoted to them that indicate a woman's position in both marriage and in the church is restricted? Is God giving a prediction or a prescription when he says to the woman in Genesis 3, "He shall rule over you?" Is that her eternal fate? Have we lost the image of God in the Fall? How does the Redeemer Jesus treat women? What are the practical implications that follow?

It is in this context that women like Bette Boersma find themselves asking questions about who God meant them to be. It takes courage to pursue this issue because many are threatened by any attempt to disturb the status quo. Sometimes men react with hostility to suggestions of equality, or women may think it unspiritual to even hint that the biblical text may contain a different interpretation. The word "feminist" becomes an accusation. Yet reality says that Truth is not weakened by investigation; it will still remain the truth that sets us free.

This book records the findings of one woman who began at the beginning and with honesty and submission to God has tried to find answers to questions the culture has dumped on her life. She has done a credible job, and her hope and mine is that reading this book might set in motion freedom for many others. Both men and women need a new understanding of a basic truth: when we affirm each other, we affirm ourselves. All of us need to know the glorious possibilities that come from being created in the image of God.

Gladys Hunt

Introduction: Is Exclusion God's Idea?

Can I believe that men and women are equal and still believe the Bible is true and it is God's Word for us today?

Many Christian women today want to believe the Bible, but they are tired of being left out. They want to be included in the decisions that affect their local church and their denomination. They want a voice and the power to effect change as it is needed. They desire the right to full participation in their religion, unhindered by exclusion policies against women.

In addition, many men see the need for women to be more involved. The task before the church is great. The harvest is plentiful, and the laborers are few (Matt 9:37). To many, it doesn't make sense to limit the field of workers and leaders by excluding those who happen to be female.

While I was growing up in church, I had little cause to question, seeing men occupy the places of power in the "big church" (the upstairs sanctuary) and women leading choruses of *Onward Christian Soldiers* downstairs in the children's Sunday School Department. Some of these same women, in fact, teaching Daily Vacation Bible School, first introduced me to the simplicity of Christ's gospel, inviting me to make it my own.

Later experiences, however, did cause me to question the maleness of this religion I had embraced. Though my parents favored a less expensive junior college, after high school I enrolled in a local Bible college, determined to pay my own way if need be. I wanted to prepare myself for a life of service to the gospel.

As a female Bible school student, however, most advisors tried to steer me into either the secretarial tract, or the Christian education tract. Neither held great interest to me. As it turned out, I opted instead for – as we used to jokingly call it—an MRS. degree. After only one year of general education and Bible classes, I married my high-school sweetheart. No one tried to dissuade me. Perhaps my advisors breathed a collective sigh of relief.

In my naivete, I persuaded my new husband into enrolling at the same Bible College in my stead. I secretly hoped God would place a calling on him—my calling, if we are to be totally honest—and I could fulfill my God-given desire for ministry vicariously through my husband.

It didn't happen. Right in the middle of Hank's first-year final exams, I was busy giving birth to our first son. For the new dad, earning a living soon took precedence over going to school and preparing for ministry, not a hard choice seeing he'd never truly been called to ministry himself.

Seventeen years and three more children later, I finally re-enrolled in college, this time the local junior college, not for my parents' sake, but in deference to our own family finances. After earning my associates' degree, I threw caution to the wind. With four kids at home, the oldest three of them teenagers, I enrolled at a nearby university and completed my bachelor's degree in just over two years.

Do you want to know the moment I'll never forget? I made a presentation in my American History class, and the professor, a retired minister, called me aside afterwards.

"Have you ever considered going into the ministry yourself?" he asked.

I cried all the way home. I still believed such doors were permanently closed to me.

I continued my education, and earned my secondary teaching certificate, mostly because I thought I needed to justify my education with the promise of gainful employment at the end of it. I majored in literature, and was struck by the virtual exclusion of women writers from the recognized canon of American and English literature.

When I finally graduated, I returned to life as a typical American housewife and mother. Teaching jobs being scarce, I eventually took a job in a large local church, writing and editing their newsletter and other print communications. Unfortunately, my experiences reinforced my discontent with the status of women in ministry. I began to seriously question the tradition of excluding women from leadership in today's church. Now, however, I was confronted with the accusation that to believe or behave otherwise was to reject the

... a great relief to discover... I could believe the Bible and also believe in the equality of men and women.

authority of the Bible. According to the Bible, my detractors said, God has ordained the authority of men and the subordination of women.

With a great deal of caution and something very close to shame, I began to ask God to help me sort out my feelings and beliefs about the role of women in the home and in the church. Why did I experience such a disconnect between what I felt deep down was right and what my Christian tradition taught as truth?

I began my search for truth with the firm belief that if I lacked wisdom, I needed only to ask God, who promises to grant it liberally and without reproach (James 1:5).

I did not, however, begin it as a quest to prove the traditional evangelical view of men and women wrong. Rather, I began with two questions. First, I wanted to know God's heart toward women. Second, I asked, "Can I love God, honor the Scriptures and still believe that men and women are equal before God, equal to serve?"

It came as a great relief to discover, after much prayer and searching, that I could indeed believe the Bible and also believe in the equality of men and women. I could believe the Bible and still believe God calls both men and women into servant leadership in the body of Christ. Even more wonderful, I came to a new awareness of God's love for me as one of his daughters.

If my discoveries are true, the implications are tremendous. Women can, after all, believe the Bible *and* be true to the calling God has put on their lives. Women *can* honor the gifts God has given them, without regard to gender, and still be true to the Scriptures that guide our lives as Christians.

The goal of this book is not to spare the reader the prayer and reflection required to know God's heart toward women in the church. It can, however, spare hours of searching and reading needed to acquire a basic understanding of biblical equality.

I have read widely both current and historic biblical scholars who have put forth their arguments thoroughly, if sometimes obscurely. I have waded through some rather formidable academic language and exhaustive research in order to glean the things I wanted to know. In *The Second Eve*, I hope to make a straightforward and careful presentation of the things I have learned. I hope to offer an introduction to the principles of Biblical Equality.

Rethinking Our Traditions

A great gulf seems to exist between the sexes. We are all part of the race called human, created in the image of God, divided along gender lines into opposites — the opposite sexes — opposing one another, often at war on either side of a great divide.

But what does God want? What did he intend for the relationship between men and women? In this day when the word "feminist" conjures up visions of rebellious women demanding their rights to promiscuity and abortion, how do we set aside our prejudices to discover what God wants for womankind, much less what he wants for an individual woman?

The world of science has begun to acknowledge once again the real and measurable differences between male and female. In the church, we rejoice when the national media reports science has "discovered" through research what believers have known all along. We have always known women and men are different by design. We trust the one who created them male and female to instruct us in how we then should live.

How well have we listened? How often have we in the body of Christ examined ourselves to see if we are truly operating by godly principles?

What if we have failed to understand God's heart because we have not sought his face or listened carefully to his words?

I began several years ago to wonder if I could, for a brief period, set aside my traditions and read God's word as a fresh new document. I decided to seek God's heart on the matter of men and women. As I mentioned, I asked God to show me His heart toward women. I did not know when I began my search if I would simply come full circle back to my currently held beliefs, or if God would show me something new.

The risky part was this: I began my search for truth about God's heart toward women before my husband, a committed traditionalist, was even aware of a problem. One thing was in my favor. After serving for years on the problem-solving team at General Motors, Hank said he'd learned that the ability to solve any problem begins with the ability to ask the right question. The question I began to ask was not, "How do we know what women may and may not do in the church?" but: "What is God's heart and desire toward women like me? How can we, as women, best fulfill our ministry in the home and in the church?"

One thing, at least, both Hank and I could agree on. If we know God's heart (thoughts, feelings, attitude) we are more likely to know what God wants us to do.

God is pleased when we seek to know him better. He promises, *"You will seek me and find me when you seek me with all your heart"* (Jer. 29:13). He also promises to give us wisdom when we ask him for it (James 1:5). We encourage you to ask.

Recently I finished reading John R.W. Stott's classic, *Basic Christianity*. He encourages his readers to seek God diligently, humbly, honestly, and obediently. I was profoundly moved by what he said about the last one. Let me share it with you:

> *We must seek obediently. This is the hardest condition of all to fulfill. In seeking God we have to be prepared not only to revise our ideas, but to reform our lives. The Christian message has a moral challenge. If the message is true, the moral challenge has to be accepted. So God is not a fit object for man's detached scrutiny. You cannot fix God at the end of a telescope or a microscope, and say 'How interesting!' God is not interesting. He is deeply upsetting. The same is true of Jesus Christ (Stott, 17).*

Looking again at God's attitude toward women may for some readers involve rethinking some deeply-held beliefs. That too can be upsetting. Hank and I sincerely hope this compilation of notes and scriptures will assist you in your search. A list of supplementary sources and books is included at the end.

For all of us, as we seek to know God's desire, may our own desire be to love the Lord our God with all our heart, soul, strength and mind (Mark 12:30).

In addition, I have asked the Lord to help me to have a "meek and quiet spirit" (1 Peter 3:4). As I have tried to know God's heart toward women, I have encountered many things that have stirred my passions. I've seen injustices against women. I have encountered accusations and misunderstandings from Christians who do not understand my quest or my reason for it. I have heard arguments for the subordination of women that are so circular they made my head spin.

Lest anyone misunderstand my desire to be meek, I'd like to

offer some information about the word. According to the Strong's dictionary, "the meek are those wholly relying on God rather than their own strength to defend them against injustice." Also, keep in mind that when the King James Bible was translated in 16th century England, "meek" was a horse training term. It meant "sensitive to the bit."

Therefore, a mighty racehorse, strong and full of vibrant energy and spirit, can increase her value by learning to be meek. The more the horse learns to anticipate the desire of her master, the more she depends on his or her leading, the more likely she is to win the race.

I have asked the Lord to help me to be sensitive to the voice of his spirit, as if it were a bit in my mouth to show me the direction and the pace he has set for me. And if there is any injustice, against me or against women in general, I am determined to rely wholly on God, rather than my own strength, to defend against it.

Meanwhile, I will do my best to serve those who read this by telling what I know and what I believe as clearly as I can and as fairly as possible.

"And the LORD answered me, and said, Write the vision, and make it plain upon tables, that he (and she) may run that reads it" (Hab. 2:2).

A Note From Hank

I have held the traditional view of restricting women from leadership positions in the church for most of my life. Several years ago my wife embarked on a quest for the truth to know the heart of God toward women. Her search challenged our traditional views. My wife has spent at least twelve years studying and praying about this issue, and during that time the two of us spent a couple of years in intensive debate over the role of women in the church. I think in time I just about wore out the word "yabut."

It didn't help that the two people in my life I considered to be the most spiritual held opposing views. They each spend hours every day in prayer and Bible study and they each truly desire to do God's will. Yet they each passionately but differently view this issue. I have studied the issue for myself, and called upon the Lord to grant me wisdom.

"If any of you lacks wisdom, he should ask God, who gives generously to all without finding fault, and it will be given to him" James 1:5, NIV.)

I have called upon the Holy Ghost to lead me to the truth ("*But when he, the Spirit of truth, comes, he will guide you into all truth*" (John 16:13).

> *As for you, the anointing you received from him remains in you, and you do not need anyone to teach you. But as his anointing teaches you about all things and as that anointing is real*" (1 John 2:27).

In terms of time, sweat, and tears, this has certainly been a most difficult, yet rewarding experience. Having come to the realization that my wife is my peer, I met a new and wonderfully exciting woman. It was a little like the time when I was born again. After all the struggle and resistance, I looked back and wondered, "Why did I wait so long?"

I never would have imagined the impact that viewing my wife as my peer instead of my subordinate would have on our relationship. It set us both free. What I hadn't realized was, in keeping my wife under the law, I had put myself under the law. Having embraced these rules of subordination, I was under constant pressure to enforce them.

Instead of freely enjoying my wife's unique personality as God designed her, I filtered everything through the gray lens of my assumed authority and leadership. Instead of enjoying her for who God created her to be, I saw all of her ideas, suggestions and disagreements through my concept of what a meek and quiet woman should be. I now feel like a veil has been removed, and I see my wife more clearly for the gifted and wise person she is.

After 36 years of marriage we have become one in a new sense of the word. I can now truly say "Many women do noble things, but you surpass them all" (Proverbs 31:29). And I understand better the command, "Give her the reward she has earned, and let her works bring her praise at the city gate" (Proverbs 31:31).

I believe the overriding principles of our new covenant with God are that we first love him with all our heart, soul, strength, and mind, and then we love our neighbors as ourselves. The women in the church are also our "neighbors" and they have been wounded by our disregard for their wisdom and their gifts. I can no longer pass by on the other side.

I think the concepts of oneness, liberty, freedom, redemption, mutual submission, and serving one another should be the healing balm for these wounded hearts. These biblical concepts should be enough to make us reevaluate restrictions on women based on gender alone.

Outside of the church, placing restrictions on people based on their gender is unethical and even illegal. In this way, the world is doing a better job of honoring women than is the church.

The word says, "There is neither Jew nor Greek, there is neither bond nor free, there is neither male nor female: for ye are all one in Christ Jesus" (Gal. 3:28). I pray we can, as men and women and as the body of Christ, move forward toward the goal of truly becoming one, so we can correctly reflect the image of God.

Hank Boersma

PART 1

Eve Introduced

Chapter~

1. Who Does She Think She Is?

Ironically, after my discouragement with being pushed toward the secretarial track in Bible College, my first part time job as a newlywed was as a secretary for my church. I left that job only to become a full-time file clerk for a larger Christian organization. All the better for our financial situation while my new husband was in Bible College, I thought. Before I had even worked to put him through his first semester, however, I discovered I was pregnant.

In the early weeks of my pregnancy, when regular morning sickness tipped my hand to my employers, my supervisor called me to her desk. It seems my Christian superiors had had a little pow-wow and decided it would be better for all concerned if I resigned. When I started to cry, she assured me the decision had nothing to do with me, or my job performance. She murmured something about company policy and appearances.

I was devastated. I remembered a Home Economics teacher from my high school who had been fired because she became pregnant out of wedlock. The school's policy aimed at removing negative examples for the students, but I remember feeling bad for the teacher's shame and loss. Now here I was, being fired for being pregnant while married. To be sure, the pregnancy was unexpected and ahead of our ideal schedule, but it had never occurred to me that I would lose my job—and my income—almost as soon as I learned the news myself.

A week or two after I was fired, I finally dried my eyes and went back to the five and dime where I had worked during high school and asked for my old job back. About halfway through my pregnancy I heard a story on the radio about a group of women who had filed and won a lawsuit against employers whose policy prevented them from working during pregnancy. I knew I could have made the same claim against the Christian company who had just let me go.

I have to admit, part of me wanted to fight back. In one part of my brain, I knew the larger issue that Christians don't sue Christians, and that individual rights are not more important than the potential ministry of a Christian organization. But I also have to admit that another, more insecure part of me, was afraid. Afraid I'd discover someone had been secretly unhappy with my work, and my pregnancy was just the excuse they needed to let me go. (This fear was not logical, nor based on any negative reviews or comments by my superiors.) Afraid I'd be labeled "trouble-maker" and have to bear the shame of standing in the way of God's work. Afraid there was some Christian reason for keeping pregnant women off the work force, and I was too ignorant of the Bible to know it yet.

I declined. I like to think my more noble ideals of ministry over personal rights prevailed. However, I also know I lacked the courage to overcome even my most irrational fears. I was certainly not ready to take on the whole Christian establishment and its apparent bias against women in the workplace. However, this first direct encounter with inequality in the workplace probably helped to set me on my course to discover God's heart for women. I sensed that something was amiss concerning the place of women within the Christian community. I felt a certain shame about this unhappiness, and I felt alone.

Apparently, though, I was not alone. Before I ever discovered a single Christian voice proclaiming the potential equality of men and women, a controversy over proper biblical gender roles had emerged among prominent Christian thinkers, scholars and writers across the nation. In fact, at least in the conservative Christian community, the controversy has materialized as a conflict between two rather distinct views. Individual beliefs may vary, but the beliefs are generally represented by one of two camps.

1. The more conservative view endorses granting males a singular leadership role in both marriage and in the church.

2. The other view rejects the notion that gender is an irrevocable determiner of leadership roles in the home and in the church.

Besides being at odds about the issue itself, unfortunately, the two camps are also at odds about the terms that best describe themselves and their opponents.

... The more conservative view endorses granting males a singular leadership role in both marriage and in the church.

Asking questions, rebellion or responsibility?

Before we identify the groups who speak for the representative viewpoints, I'd like to look at the nature of controversy within various factions of Christianity.

Some consider it rebellion to question traditionally held beliefs about women in the church. My sincere desire to please God has given me cause to question it myself. But God says if I lack wisdom, I can ask God directly, and I will receive it generously, without reproach. Men and women have reproached me. God has been true to his word. He has not reproached me for asking him to show me his heart toward women. And every day he shows me a little more.

I've wandered around a little during my search. I've looked at things from different angles. I've seen things in the Bible I didn't know were there. I've imagined things that weren't. But since the day I first dared to ask the question, "Lord, will you please show me your heart toward women?" my life has become richer, my relationship with God has grown sweeter, and some of the barriers have come down, barriers that once separated me from a truly wonderful and honest relationship with my husband, and even barriers that kept me from understanding what God thinks about racism, sexism, and class distinctions.

Once the South was full of wealthy plantation owners who treated their slaves with a certain amount of dignity and kindness. Because of their benevolence, they couldn't understand all the fuss about freedom. They defended their right to own slaves on biblical grounds, but completely missed caring about the right of a slave to be free. A century later, when Dr. Martin Luther King crusaded for the civil rights of blacks, many white Christians called him a rebel

... The other view rejects the notion that gender is an irrevocable determiner of leadership roles in the home and in the church.

and a Communist. When people acted on their conscience to take action against discrimination, they too were accused of rebellion. Dr. King rallied his followers by encouraging non-violent protests and forgiveness for their oppressors.

Revival brings down barriers

Did you know that the first feminist movement in America, the one that finally gave women the vote in 1918, began as a direct result of The Second Great Awakening?

The revival that swept the nation in the late 1820's and 30's, mostly because of the work of one Charles Finney, spawned a major reform movement. Women who were newly born again and empowered by the Holy Spirit, started to set some very wrong things right. They campaigned against liquor and prostitution, against debtor's prisons and against slavery. Christian women began to wield power and influence over the moral conditions of society by enlisting the support of churches, by bringing publicity to their causes, and by their own powers of persuasion. In 1840 a group of American anti-slavery advocates traveled to the world-wide anti-slavery convention in London. The women in their party were denied entrance to the convention, simply because they were women.

As a result of the barriers Christian women encountered when they sought to fully participate in moral reform, another social reform movement shifted into high gear. This time women, like Elizabeth Cady Stanton, Susan B. Anthony, Lucy Stone and Lucretia Mott, fought to change their own legal and social status in order to empower themselves for the good of society. Many Christian women helped to lead the quest for the right of women to vote — as a tool to help them bring about positive moral change in a corrupt society.

The second feminist movement in America sprang up hand-in-hand with the Civil Rights movement of the 1960's. When the spotlight shown on the lack of equality for blacks, the light also exposed an inequality between men and women. A changing economy was pushing women into the work-force where pay and working conditions were not always favorable to the fairer sex. Women who became aware of the cultural inequities between genders worked hard to raise the consciousness of other women to their plight.

Anger and bitterness build walls

What began as a need for awareness and change became fueled by a groundswell of anger and bitterness. The problems may have been real enough, but for many, anger and resentment prevailed over grace and forgiveness. As a result, the second wave of feminism in America became marked by sin. Today the word "feminist" conjures up visions of rebellious women demanding their right to promiscuity and abortion, instead of women seeking the power needed to combat wickedness and promote righteousness.

I discovered my own tendency toward anger and resentment at various times as I studied the history of attitudes and actions toward women. Like this fact: the slaves were freed in the 1860's, but the women who fought for them didn't win voting rights until 1918. I could get hot over that. But God, who never restricted me from learning, has warned me sternly about anger and bitterness. Forgiveness and grace are better. Not because I am a woman, but because I am one of his, and even if I know all the answers about the women's issue, but have not love, I am nothing. I will become like a clanging symbol., full of annoyance, but with no fruit.

The Big Question

When people hear rumors that Hank and I have been studying "the woman issue," someone always asks *The Big Question*: "Do you believe a woman can be a senior pastor?"

I have trouble understanding the apparent significance of the question, or why the questioner seems so threatened by the possible answer. I wonder sometimes if they think a woman is lurking behind every pulpit in America, preparing to take over as soon as I give the word.

The answer to the question is one of calling. Since I believe men and women are equal before God, I believe God can call a woman to a place of authority as well as a man. I believe neither a man nor a woman should presume to teach or to exercise authority unless God is behind it. I do not think that every woman is called to be a pastor, any more than I believe every man is so called.

But how could I say that God could never call a woman to be a senior pastor? First, how can I presume to know what God will or will not do? And second, which of Christ's

... "Do you believe a woman can be a senior pastor?"

"joint heirs" am I willing to disqualify from the gifts and calling of God?

But perhaps I'm getting ahead of myself. The following chapters will help show how I have come to believe in biblical equality, and why. For the sake of this writing, it is imperative to understand that the controversy is not between people who believe the Bible and people who do not. It is not between people who wish to remain faithful to God and his Word and those who would rather choose a more liberal and modern way of life. Rather, it is between faithful Christians who differ about how the message of the Bible speaks to the role of males and females.

I know what you think, but what do you call yourself?

As we said before, besides being at odds about the role of males and females, unfortunately, the two camps are also at odds about the terms that best describe themselves and their opponents.

Traditionalist or Evangelical Feminist

Since the group assigning leadership roles to males and subordinate or helper roles to females follows the more traditional pattern of beliefs and practices, it has often been labeled ***traditionalist***. On the other hand, those Christians who believe traditional restrictions on the roles of women should be lifted have been called ***evangelical feminists***.

As a rule, the people who hold to one view or the other do so with passion and conviction. Unfortunately, some have also resorted to name-calling—not the childish kind, but the political kind. Just as the news media can't resist selecting loaded terms to describe a favored or disfavored party or candidate, neither side of the gender issue has fully resisted communicating its own bias by the labels it chooses.

Both terms, "traditionalist" and "feminist," can be seen as loaded guns. Objections to the term *traditionalist* stem from the implication that this group honors its traditions above the Bible. Some worry the title may even suggest the religious traditionalism of the Pharisees, which Jesus condemned. Although people in this camp do hold the more traditional view of male and female roles, they also believe theirs is the biblical position. They do not want the fact that their view is supported by centuries of tradition to weaken their biblical stand.

The second group may not raise loud objections to the title evangelical feminist, but the negative connotations inherent in the word feminist are unavoidable. Feminism conjures up images of bra-burning angry women demanding equal rights

... As a rule, the people who hold to one view or the other do so with passion and conviction.

to promiscuity and power. It calls up the whole debate over reproductive rights and abortion. I'd rather refer to this group as the supporters of biblical equality between men and women, and not associate them with rebels against society's accepted norms or promoters of abortion rights.

We are left to decide, for the sake of discussion and brevity, what we will call each view and its party. Since those who advocate male leadership are indeed following the more traditional interpretation of Scriptures, during this discussion their views will be called traditional, and the followers, for lack of a better term, will be called traditionalists. The traditional view is the one that, based on a particular interpretation of Scriptures, assigns women a subordinate and secondary role in the family and in the church. The term allows us to understand that this view has been more prominently represented by the beliefs and practices of the church for centuries. The use of the term is not intended to denigrate the position or its followers.

Those who advocate an equal playing field between men and women for the selection of leaders shall be called egalitarians. The egalitarian view is the one, based on a different interpretation of scriptures, which removes traditional restrictions on the role of women in the church and supports equality and mutual submission within the family.

Complimentarian

A third term is often thrown into the mix. A significant controversy has brewed over the use of the term **"complimentarian."** Traditionalists have stated a preference to use this term to describe their position. With it they attempt to say they believe men and women are equal before God and their *biblically-assigned roles* are complimentary to one another.

The problem with this title and definition is simply this: Both groups claim to believe that men and women are equal before God and serve complimentary roles in the family, the church and society. The difference is in how the two groups understand the matter of biblically assigned roles.

The distinction comes down to **how** the equality of men and women is expressed in our daily lives. One group proposes that while men and women are "equal in being," the Bible demands they maintain distinct roles. This group assigns leadership and authority in the home and the church exclusively and permanently to one of the so-called equal sides. It assigns a permanent subordinate role of service to the other of the "equal" sides. This is, of course, the traditional view.

The egalitarian group, on the other hand, believes the Bible emphasizes the unity and oneness of believers, giving rise to an equality of persons which does *not* demand separate roles based on gender, race or class distinctions. As Rebecca Merrill Groothuis emphasizes in her book *Good News for Women*, the claim of traditionalists that women are "equal in being" while subject to "a lifelong subordination that is determined by a person's inherent nature," (namely, femaleness) is less than logical. The claim may deflect attention from the implied inferiority of women inherent in the traditional position, but it does not resolve the issue.

Who really cares?

Christians have been reading the Bible to determine how to live for centuries. It is an understatement to say not all Christians agree about how to interpret and apply the words of the Bible. Only with significant hubris does any group make an exclusive claim to truth.

However, it will help to know a little bit about the groups and writings that represent the two opposing viewpoints.

The Traditional View: The Council on Biblical Manhood and Womanhood (CBMW)

In support of differing roles for men and women in the home and church, The Council on Biblical Manhood and Womanhood (CBMW) is based in Louisville, Ky. The CBMW believes that men and women are essentially equal in a spiritual sense, but in the church and the home, men are to hold the leadership positions, and women are to graciously submit to that leadership.

Some of those who hold the traditional view have compiled a fairly thorough and scholarly look at their position in a book called *Recovering Biblical Manhood & Womanhood, A Response to Evangelical Feminism*, edited by John Piper and Wayne Grudem (Crossway Books, Wheaton. 1991). Notice how the title illustrates an earlier statement about communicating bias. As stated earlier, the conflict is not between one group who believes and obeys the Bible and one group who does not.

The terminology, "Recovering Biblical Manhood & Womanhood" clouds the issue. Manhood and womanhood are defined in Webster's as "the state of being a man (woman); manly (womanly) qualities; men (women) collectively." Neither manhood nor womanhood is at issue in the debate between egalitarians and traditionalists. Whether a man or woman believes the Bible supports equal or traditional roles for men and women does not in any way determine that person's manhood or womanhood.

Using the word "Recovering" implies that something, namely manhood, womanhood or the Bible, has been lost. The truth is, those who believe in the biblical equality of men and women do not challenge either the authority of the Bible or biblical manhood and womanhood. Egalitarians have rejected a traditional interpretation of the Bible that uses gender as a basis for assigning leadership roles, but they have not rejected biblical manhood and womanhood.

One dedicated Christian man I know, when confronted with the title, *Recovering Biblical Manhood & Womanhood*, declared, "I will not have my "manhood" defined in terms of how well I subordinate the women in my life!"

The Egalitarian View: Christians for Biblical Equality (CBE)

There is a growing contingency of "Bible-believing Christians" who support the equality of men and women in both principle and in the assigning of roles. While this book serves as an introduction to principles of that equality, the body of work supporting an egalitarian and biblical view of male and female relationships is growing fast (See Bibliography).

In support of treating men and women equally in roles and relationships, Christians for Biblical Equality (CBE) is based in Minneapolis. CBE is made up of men and women from many denominations

"... who believe that the Bible, properly interpreted, teaches the fundamental equality of men and women of all racial and ethnic groups and all economic classes, based on the teachings of Scripture as reflected in Galatians 3:28: There is neither Jew nor Greek, there is neither slave nor free, there is neither male nor female; for you are all one in Christ Jesus*"(CBE International web site, at cbeinternational.org.)*

Of course, numerous other organizations exist to promote the equal participation of women in culture and religion. A key-word search on the Internet will bring up many additional resources. CBE is singled out here because its values and statement of belief, except in regard to male/female roles, match closely those of other conservative Christian groups, including those of CBMW.

Chapter~

2. First Adam and First Eve

The same American History professor who asked me if I'd ever considered going into the ministry also first exposed me to the names Sarah and Angelina Grimke. Both women fought avidly for the abolition of slavery, and were among the first female public speakers in America. As such, they came under strong attack and criticism from the church. In her 1838 response, Sarah wrote what became known as *Letters on the Equality of the Sexes*, in which she defended women's right to the public platform.

The professor, a retired Reformed minister, did not hesitate to point out Sarah's radical statement that, according to the Genesis account of creation, both men and women were equally created in the image of God. It was, he said, a remarkable discovery on her part, because although it was a correct rendering of the text, it ran contrary to the beliefs and practices of the religious culture of the day, which sought to confine women to the silent space within the homes of husbands or fathers.

Even though by this time in my life I had participated in numerous Bible studies, read many religious texts and heard countless sermons, still, in my nearly four decades of church membership, this was the very first time I'd heard anything like this. I had been a Christian since my childhood, yet it was the first time I'd heard *anybody* suggest that I, as woman, had been created in the image of God.

I felt cautious at first, determined to study it out for myself so as not to be deceived. As I began to see that Sarah Grimke just might be on to something, I felt a mixture of betrayal and elation, the one because this treasure of information had been kept from me, and the other because God had not disregarded me.

If Sarah Grimke was right, then I, a woman, had been made just as much in God's image as any man had been. No wonder I needed to search it out for myself. Following the good problem solving principle I learned from my traditionalist-husband, I sought first to ask the right questions. Besides the obvious, "Can I really believe that I, a woman, am formed in the image of God?" I approached my rereading of the Genesis account of creation looking for the answer to these two questions: "What *does* it say about God's intent for men and women?" and, contrary to what I have believed, "What does it *not* say?

What the original creation account says:

Many of the arguments for the traditional view on men and women go back to the story of creation as recorded in the book of Genesis. The hierarchal understanding of the relationship between men and women stems, at least in part, from some commonly held notions about the creation of Adam and Eve. Here let's look at some things the Genesis account truly does say:

Male and female were made in the image of God.

Genesis 1 gives an account of each day of creation. On the sixth day, after God made every kind of animal, he made a man and a woman. Let's look again at this part of the creation account recorded in Genesis 1:26-28:

> *"And God said, Let us make man in our image, after our likeness: and let them have dominion over the fish of the sea, and over the fowl of the air, and over the cattle, and over all the earth, and over every creeping thing that creepeth upon the earth. So God created man in his own image, in the image of God created he him; male and female created he them. And God blessed them, and God said unto them, Be fruitful, and multiply, and replenish the earth, and subdue it: and have dominion over the fish of the sea, and over the fowl of the air, and over every living thing that moveth upon the earth."*

Two things are evident here, namely, God created them, male and female, in his image, and he gave them, male and female, dominion or leadership over the rest of creation.

In "Let us make man in our image," the Hebrew word translated *man* is *adam*, not Adam the man, but adam, a generic term to describe human beings or humankind.

" ... and God said to them ...have dominion ..."

"In our likeness," God said. "Let us make man (humankind) in our image, after our likeness." As if to clear up any notion that God is just talking about making males, the passage repeats, "male and female created he them ... and God said to them... have dominion ..."

The passage, in fact, contains some very interesting uses of plural and singular pronouns for both God and man. The completeness of God is expressed in God's statement "Let us make man in our image." We know "the Lord our God is one God," and it is generally understood that the plurality here refers to the persons of the Godhead, Father, Son and Spirit. God, who refers to himself in the plural (us, our) also refers to his creation of humankind in the plural (them). "And God said, 'Let us (God) make man (them) in our image." "Male and female created he them."

Egalitarian Christians believe Genesis 1 clearly tells us God did not make man (male) in his image, he made **humankind** (male and female together) in his image.

Those who believe God intended males to occupy a permanent and pervasive position of authority and leadership over women, commonly understand the story as follows: Adam, or the male part of humankind, was created first. It is assumed that Adam, the man (male) was created in God's image, and except for his loneliness and need of a helper, he was complete and able to fully reflect the image of God. Adam, the man, was given dominion over the earth and the rest of the animal kingdom. Once God realized that Adam might need a companion, the traditional story goes, he fashioned Eve, a helper fit for him.

The egalitarian understanding of the relationship between men and women looks at the creation story differently. Those who believe that God created male and female to be equal, believe God created humankind, male and female, to be like God and to have dominion over the rest of creation. There is no indication in these verses that males are made any more in God's image than are females. Neither is there any indication that dominion over other living things is given any more to males than females.

It takes both male and female to complete the Image of God.

It takes both male and female together in order to express the image of God. Man (male) alone was not sufficient. In fact, in the creation account in Genesis 2, God said, "It is not good for the man (the individual male) to be alone."

As noted earlier, man or adam in Genesis 1:26 can be translated *human,* or *humankind,* as it represents both male and female. Genesis 2 contains a separate, more detailed account of the creation of humankind. In this account we learn of the garden prepared for man, and we see Adam the man as a solitary being, beginning to tend the garden and give names to the animals. God saw that Adam was alone and declared his state "not good."

One way to bring the two accounts together is to see the original creation of man as one body that enclosed both male and female. This may or may not be the case, but it's one possible explanation of the presence of both male and female in Genesis 1. While some scholars see in the first two chapters of Genesis two different accounts of the events of creation, with the second account going into greater detail concerning the creation of Adam and Eve, other scholars believe that adam (humankind), as originally created, contained both male and female.

In this approach, when God sees that man alone is not good, He separates the feminine from the masculine in order to form a complimentary helper and mate for the man.

Looking at the text, at the end of the sixth day, according to chapter one, God looked at his creation and said it was good. In chapter two, however, *"The LORD God said, 'It is **not good** for the man to be alone . . .'"* (Genesis 2:18).

From Adam's rib, God formed the woman. And the man said, *"This is now bone of my bones, and flesh of my flesh: she shall be called Woman, because she was taken out of man"* (2:23).

Together, Adam and the woman were more like God than Adam had been alone. Adam alone was **not good**. God is good.

A friend of mine, Dr. Bill Beebe, shared these thoughts with me. God formed Eve, he said, not as an after-thought when he saw how alone and needy Adam was. Instead, God planned Eve as an expression of communion. Genesis speaks of seven days of creation. All was accomplished in the first six days. On the seventh day, God rested and had communion with his creation. God sees that all is good, but in the spirit of communion, one thing is not good. Adam is alone. So God brought a deep (Sabbath) rest upon Adam and separated Eve from him as an expression of Adam's glory. Now Adam, like God, could say that it was good. In Eve, Adam could be complete.

Gilbert Bilezikian, in his book, *Community 101*, says God declared the being he created to reflect his image "to be 'not good' because it was solitary. The reason for God's displeasure was this: as a solitary individual, Adam "had no oneness." We know God as Trinity. "Therefore, the creation in his image required the creation of a plurality of persons. God's supreme achievement was not the creation of a solitary man, but the creation of the human community" (page 19).

Together, Adam and Eve were more like God than Adam had been alone. This is not a declaration that only married individuals can reflect God's image. It is instead a declaration that God intends us human beings to live together in community. Genesis 1 and 2 assure us that the community of God includes both male and female. The New testament writings of Paul make sure we understand the community includes all who are in Christ Jesus, without distinctions or exclusions due to race, social class or gender. (See Galatians 3:28.)

A man and wife as "one flesh" -- an expression of the Image of God.

The New Testament confirms the oneness God intended in Mark 10: 6-8:

> *But from the beginning of the creation God made them male and female. For this cause shall a man leave his father and mother, and cleave to his wife; And they twain shall be one flesh: so then they are no more twain, but one flesh (Mark 10:6-8).*

Please trust that I am not suggesting single and/or childless people are in any way less an expression of the image of God. However, it is clear from many scriptures, one good and God-like thing about man and woman together is their ability to *"Be fruitful, and multiply, and replenish the earth,"* as man alone could never do. The union of male and female in marriage gives us a picture of the ideal union between God and man. This is something God wants us to understand, whether we are married or single.

*"For we are all members of his body. 'For this reason a man
will leave his father and mother and be united to his wife,
and the two will become one flesh.' This is a profound
mystery - but I am talking about Christ and the church"
(Eph. 5:30-32).*

*"Yet for us there is but one God, the Father, from whom all
things came and for whom we live; and there is but one
Lord, Jesus Christ, through whom all things came and
through whom we live" (1 Cor. 8:6).*

God, referred to in the plural (*Let us make man in our image*) is,
nevertheless, one God. In similar fashion, while God caused men
and women to become separate individual beings, he also insti-
tuted marriage and commanded that the two be joined together
again as one flesh. It is only when the two become one that their
union brings forth life in the form of conception and childbirth. In
order to be like God and bring forth life, a man and a woman must
become ONE (like God).

God created Adam and Eve. He told them to *"Be fruitful, and
multiply, and replenish the earth"* (Gen. 1:28). God passed the work
of creation on to the ones he had made in his image, but only as
they became **one** could they fulfill this creative command.

(Jesus said) *"I and the Father are one"* (John 10:30). God ordains
male and female (plural) become one in marriage, which we know
is part of the mystery, a picture of Christ and the church. We know
from the prayer of Jesus in John 17, *"that they may be one, as we are
one,"* the unity of being one with God and with one another is
God's desire.

On the division threatened between Jewish believers and non-
Jewish believers, the apostle Paul encouraged oneness with
language that calls to mind the oneness God intends between a
man and woman when they become one in marriage.

*For he himself is our peace, who has made the two one and
has destroyed the barrier, the dividing wall of hostility, by
abolishing in his flesh the law with its commandments and
regulations. His purpose was to create in himself **one new
man*** out of the two, thus making peace, and in this **one
body** to reconcile both of them to God through the cross, by
which he put to death their hostility (Eph. 2:14-16, NIV).*

*Humanity, in Ephesians 2, is probably a more accurate rendering of the word "anthropos" translated "one new man" in the *King James* and *New International Version*. It means human being, whether male or female. The *New Revised Standard* version and the *Today's New International Version* use the word "humanity" here. *The Living Bible* and *The New Living Translation* use the word "person." In any case, the meaning is not "man as in human male" but person, human being, or humanity as a whole.

Though this passage speaks of non-Jews and Jews, I have come to believe God means it to apply to the reconciliation between male and female as well. Oneness, whether between male and female, Jew and Greek, slave and free person, reflects God's desire. (See John 17:11 and Galatians 3:28).

After exploring what it says, I looked again to find out what it does not say:

What the original creation account does not say:

Some of my early misconceptions about the nature of the relationship between men and women stemmed from my own misunderstanding of the story of creation. I inherited beliefs from the creation story that were not, in reality, part of the story. As I sought to know God's heart toward women, I struggled especially with some New Testament passages that seemed to settle the issue before I had a chance to study them in depth.

I discovered one important thing early on. In order to correctly interpret important New Testament Scriptures about men and women in the church, I first had to understand what God intended for men and women in creation. That meant undoing some common misconceptions about the original creation story.

The order of creation does not suggest even a hint of superiority of the male over the female part of creation.

The order of creation (Adam was created first, then Eve) does not in itself suggest the superiority of Adam. Because the creation of humankind is the last act of creation, we usually assume creation progressed from the least to the greatest. No one assumes that because the animals were created before Eve, the animals are therefore superior to Eve. It is just as illogical to assume Adam's superiority because he appears before Eve. At least in theory, if the order of creation was moving from least to greatest, then the order of creation suggests God saved the best for last.

Some scholars and writers who study the original languages of the account say the language in both the Hebrew and Greek texts stress the equality and similarity of Adam and Eve, not the inequality and the superiority of Adam. In fact, looking at the grammar of the phrase "helper fit for him," provides at least the slightest hint of Eve's superiority. "Fit for him" means "in front of" or "visible to" Adam. The same term is used to describe David's rule over Israel in Psalms 89:19. (For more information, see the book, *Beyond the Curse* by Aida and David Spencer.)

The term "help-meet" does not imply a God ordained hierarchy between men and women.

She is called a "helper fit for him." Helper here does not in any way imply a subordinate assistant. The word for helper is "ezer" and out of twenty-one appearances in the Old Testament, fifteen times the word refers to God* (see list of references below.) It speaks of God as helper of humanity, the one who assists the desperate and helpless ones. It implies Eve was a help to Adam as God is a help to humankind.

*The word for helper (ezer) refers to God in these passages: Exo. 18:4, Deu. 33:7, Deu. 33:26, Deu. 33:29, Psa. 20:2, Psa. 33:20, Psa. 70:5, Psa. 89:19, Psa. 115:9, Psa. 115:10, Psa. 115:11, Psa. 121:1, Psa. 121:2, Psa. 124:8, Psa. 146:5, Hos. 13:9

Genesis 2:23 shows Adam's joy, with no hint of authoritarianism: And Adam said, 'This is now bone of my bones, and flesh of my flesh: she shall be called Woman, because she was taken out of Man.'

The woman was not given **to** the man for him to possess, but given **to be with** the man. Those are the words Adam himself used to describe Eve to God after he tasted the forbidden fruit: "*And the man said, The woman whom thou gavest to **be with** me, she gave me of the tree, and I did eat* (Gen. 3:12). In fact, she was "created not to serve Adam, but to serve *with* Adam" (Spencer 27).

The emphasis seems to be that God gave Adam work to do. Then he said, "It is not good for him to be alone." So he gave Adam a helper to do the work with him. Adam's aloneness was **more than loneliness**. He needed a helper. "Consequently, God says: 'I will make for him a helper equal to him.'" (see Hayter, 102 and Spencer 26-29).

Although Eve came from Adam's rib, it doesn't say women are derivative (merely an outgrowth of man) rather than autonomous (independent and self-governing) individuals.

As Mary Hayter points out in *The New Eve In Christ*, autonomy for either man or woman is a misnomer. Both receive their very existence from God and are responsible to God for their actions. The fact that woman was made from the rib of the man should signify God's intention for their unity. She became "bone of his bone" because God intended that they be joined again as one. Together they were to express the image of God.

Some have ascribed superiority to Adam because Adam names Eve. In Genesis 2:23, however, he calls her woman. He is not claiming his superiority over her. Rather he is "rejoicing in their mutuality." In other words, he proclaims her to be, unlike the animals, a proper mate for him, because she is like him (Hayter, 100-101).

It doesn't say biological or psychological differences define sex roles.

There is instead an implied co-operation between Adam and Eve, a shared responsibility and shared authority. This is not to say there is no difference between women and men. It merely says the creation account in Genesis 1 and 2 does not assign different roles to men and women based on their physical, mental, or spiritual differences. Remember, they were given authority over the garden as a shared responsibility (Gen. 1:26-28).

Understanding what the Genesis account does not say is important if we are to understand God's heart toward women. Teachers may be tempted to apply human logic to some traditional views on women and draw conclusions not born out in Scripture.

Chapter~

3. Fallen Adam and Fallen Eve

I admit, I picked up a copy of Mary Pipher's book, *Reviving Ophelia, Saving the Selves of Adolescent Girls*, because the cover copy brought tears to my eyes. I can't explain it, but it seemed an intuitive response, both to my own experience and in sympathy with my daughter, who had just finished high school. "An eye-opening look at the everyday dangers of being young and female, and how adults can help," it said. Reading the rest of the text did not diminish the powerful emotions of my first encounter.

Pipher documents for her readers the hurdles girls encounter when moving from childhood to womanhood. On page 39, she draws this startling conclusion: "Adolescent girls discover that it is impossible to be both feminine and adult."

Immediately, I thought of 1 Corinthians 13:11: When I was a child, I talked like a child, I thought like a child, I reasoned like a child. When I became a man, I put childish ways behind me.

What do we do when we become women, I wondered? Do we put away childish things and become adults? Or do we settle for a misconstrued image of femininity, and sacrifice our adulthood to it? In order to be adults, must we, as women, give up at least a portion of the image of femininity that seems so desirable in our culture?

Pipher cites a "now classic study" by Psychologist I. K. Broverman in which practicing psychologists, both male and female, were asked to check off the characteristics they saw in: -*Healthy Men*, -*Healthy Adults*, and -*Healthy Women*.

For the first two categories, *Healthy Men,* and *Healthy Adults,* the majority chose the same adjectives, including "active," "independent" and "logical." However, for the third category, *Healthy Women,* most described them with such adjectives as "passive," "dependant," and "illogical." (Irrational Beliefs Test, IBT, Jones, 1969.)

"What am I?" I wondered aloud as I read, to God or anyone who was listening, "A healthy adult, or a so-called "healthy woman"? Do I dare to behave as a healthy adult, to be active, independent and logical in my daily relationships?"

To what extent have I, and for that matter have a majority of women, chosen to be, or appear to be, childlike in order to satisfy a cultural demand to appear more feminine? How often do we take on a passive, dependant persona? How often have we allowed ourselves to be labeled illogical as part of the so-called feminine mystique? Who after all, can ever really understand a woman?

The Bible seems to describe the healthy Christian adult in Second Timothy 1:7: *"For God hath not given us the spirit of fear; but of power, and of love, and of a sound mind."* I soundly reject any notion that this promise extends exclusively to men. Yet the professionals in Broverman's study certainly did not ascribe the qualities of power and soundness of mind to their "passive, dependent, and illogical" women patients. Can I claim them for myself, I wondered? Or is it culturally still too masculine for a woman to talk of power and a sound mind?

How will I be perceived if I plant my feet firmly on the logical and biblical belief that men and women have equal claim to power and soundness of mind?

Admittedly, Broverman's study dealt with professional attitudes over 30 years ago. Hopefully these irrational beliefs have changed positively in the interim, especially in the world of educated professionals. However, I fear the same positive change still eludes many parts of the Christian community. I see in the evangelical church a cultural tendency to ascribe qualities like power, assertiveness and soundness of mind more readily to males. Some will even use this irrational belief to justify the denial of leadership roles for women.

The Scriptures which promise power and soundness of mind, along with the ones commanding us to study, gain knowledge and wisdom, be strong in the Lord, and put on the mind of Christ are addressed to all who would follow Christ, without regard to gender, nationality, or class. Biblically, then, some cultural ideas can be confidently refuted. Even if culturally some people still see women as somehow less adult, less independent, less logical, less active than men, these ideas are not born out by biblical or spiritual wisdom.

Why does this cultural bias against women persist in many areas of evangelical and conservative, traditional Christianity? I believe just as certain misunderstandings about the created nature of men and women contribute to cultural bias against women, so do misunderstandings about what happened in the Fall.

When Adam and Eve sinned in the garden, it changed their relationship to God and to each other. In this chapter, I want to re-examine the Genesis account of the consequences of sin in the Garden.

The woman sinned first

According to the Genesis 3 account of the fall, Eve sinned first. However, both Adam and Eve sinned, and both are held accountable. Some argue Eve's sin demonstrates her weakness and inferiority. However, before jumping to such an unwarranted conclusion, I'd like to examine again the temptation of Eve.

In Genesis 3:1, Satan, as the serpent, first approached Eve for the purpose of tempting her. I'd like to look at this event as one of three recorded incidents in the Bible where Satan's words and actions play a role in human history.

In the book of Job, Satan approaches God in heaven and asks permission to test the loyalty of Job, God's faithful servant. God holds Job up as a primary example of an upright man who fears God and shuns evil (Job 1:8). In the Gospels of Matthew and Luke, Satan approaches Jesus for the purpose of tempting him.

No one would suggest that Satan's strategy in approaching Jesus had anything to do with the weakness or inferiority of the one being tempted. Neither the testing of Job nor the temptation of Jesus suggests Satan's tendency to approach the weak or the inferior.

In fact, as Christians, we are often exhorted to pray for our leaders. Satan, our enemy, we are told, will often attack the leaders of a church or ministry. Leaders are vulnerable to Satan's attack, not because of weakness or inferiority, but because of their potential to damage the cause of Christ should they fall. If a leader falls, others will follow. It is often the person's position of leadership that makes him or her a target of the enemy.

In Genesis 3, Satan came to Eve with his temptation. In Matthew and Luke, he came to Jesus. Because we understand who Jesus is, we understand why Satan would target him with temptation. I believe it is only a profound misunderstanding of Eve and who God intended her to be that causes people to assume her weakness and inferiority invited Satan's attack.

The assumption does not appear to come from the evidence of Scriptures. The Scriptures, in fact, suggest the clever serpent chooses to invest his craftiness wisely. In Eve's case, his plan worked perfectly. Once the serpent managed to beguile Eve, Adam came along without so much as an argument.

If Adam were truly superior, would he not have resisted eating the fruit offered by Eve? One New Testament verse (1 Timothy 2:14) tells us that Eve was deceived and Adam was not. However, we are never told Adam's thoughts as he took the fruit from Eve and ate it. I have heard many assumptions. If Adam was not deceived, we can assume he sinned knowingly. However, we do not know if it was a sacrificial act, or a thoughtless or willful act of disobedience.

What if it was an act of submission? Perhaps Adam's desire was for his wife, and he allowed her to rule over him. Would this not have provided a fitting parallel consequence for God to then say to the woman in Genesis 3:16, "...and thy desire shall be to thy husband, and he shall rule over thee"?

Can we assume that Adam would have fared any better had the tempter come to him first? And if Satan had beguiled Adam first, how do we know Adam could have convinced his wife to partake?

The serpent came to Eve, and she was deceived. In spite of her deception, though, Eve still made a conscious choice to disobey God's command. And even though some New Testament passages refer to death and sin entering through the first Adam (Romans 5:14-15), they do not say Adam failed in his responsibility to keep his wife in line. Her sin was her responsibility. His sin was his responsibility. God addressed each of them individually to tell them the consequences of their individual sin.

No curse pronounced on the male or the female

Only the serpent and the ground are cursed. In Genesis 3, God addresses the man, the woman and the serpent, in order to tell them what will happen because of the incident in the Garden.

God asked Adam, *"Where are you?"*(3:9).

Adam admits he hid because he was ashamed and naked. And God asks directly, *"Have you eaten of the tree?"*

God asks Eve, *"What is it you have done?"* (3:13).

Eve responds, *"The serpent beguiled me and I did eat,"*

God does not ask the serpent any questions. He takes Eve's word for it, and says to the serpent on her behalf,

> *"Because thou hast done this, thou art cursed above all cattle, and above every beast of the field ..."* (3:14).

God says, in essence, I know what you did, and these are the consequences. God describes to the serpent his curse, namely that he will crawl on his belly and eat dust all his life. God also promises to put enmity between the serpent and the seed of the woman.

After cursing the serpent, God addresses the woman about the consequences of her sin:

> *Unto the woman he said, I will greatly multiply thy sorrow and thy conception; in sorrow thou shalt bring forth children; and thy desire shall be to thy husband, and he shall rule over thee.* (3:16)

To the man, God says,

> *"Because thou hast hearkened unto the voice of thy wife, and hast eaten of the tree, of which I commanded thee, saying, Thou shalt not eat of it: cursed is the ground for thy sake; in sorrow shalt thou eat of it all the days of thy life; Thorns also and thistles shall it bring forth to thee; and thou shalt eat the herb of the field; In the sweat of thy face shalt thou eat bread, till thou return unto the ground; for out of it wast thou taken: for dust thou art, and unto dust shalt thou return"* (17-19).

Note that it says the *ground* will be cursed for Adam's sake, just as it appears the serpent was cursed for Eve's. The result of sin is devastating to both Adam and Eve, but God placed neither under a curse.

Sin interferes with the creative process. Adam and Eve had been told to be fruitful and multiply. Now the fruitfulness of the womb, on Eve's part, will be hampered by pain and sorrow, and her labor will be increased. The fruitfulness of the earth, on Adam's part, will be hindered by thorns and thistles. Now as he tills the ground and harvests food, it will be by the sweat of his face (See Spencer, p. 38-39).

Sin also dramatically changes the relationship between the woman and her husband. Now, instead of ruling over God's creation with Adam, God informs Eve, "*thy desire shall be to thy husband, and he shall rule over thee.*" Even though bearing children will bring her pain and sorrow, still by her own desire, she will be subject to her husband's will. As a result of the fall, the woman becomes subservient to her husband, and he becomes domineering over her. Eve went from ruling with Adam to being ruled by him.

God describes the relationship of the man and the woman

I believe Gen. 3:16 is descriptive, not prescriptive. In other words, by saying what "shall be," God does not command either men or women to behave a certain way. Instead, he describes the way the relationship will change now that Adam and Eve have sinned and caused a rift between themselves and God.

For one thing, desire is not the kind of thing that can be commanded. God tells Eve that her desire will be to her husband, and he will rule over her. Nowhere do we read a command addressed to Adam that he should rule over his wife.

Just as some of us have presumed God pronounced a curse on Adam and Eve, even though the text does not state it, we have also assumed God's declaration of what will happen as a result of their sin became somehow a *command* that it be so. While God does *describe* what the relationship between man and woman will be after the fall, He does not necessarily *prescribe* the relationship. In other words, Genesis 3:16 offers us a good picture of what the relationship between husbands and wives will be. It does not, however, demand that we pattern our relationships thus.

Perhaps this will be easier to understand if we look at God's words to Adam about the consequences of his sin. He says thorns and thistles will grow and "*thou shalt eat the herb of the field*" (18). Should we presume God is commanding Adam, and thereby all mankind, to never again eat the fruit that grows on trees? If we must presume a command to Eve and to all women in 3:16, must we also presume the command in 3:18 for Adam and all men to eat only vegetables? Scriptural evidence demonstrates God's people

ate meats and fruits in abundance. Listen to the blessing and pro-
vision God promised for the Sabbath and Jubilee years:

> *And the land shall yield her fruit, and ye shall eat your fill,*
> *and dwell therein in safety* (Lev. 25:19.)

It is not difficult to find other examples in Genesis where the
text states what shall be. In 4:12-14, after Cain killed his brother,
God describes to Cain the consequences of his sin. *"You shall be a
fugitive and a vagabond,"* he tells him. It is not a command, "Go out
now and become a vagabond," but rather an accurate description
of the life Cain will live. Neither do we read this passage to say
that any man who kills his brother or speaks evil against his brother
(see Matthew 5:22) must thenceforth adopt the life-style of a vagabond. There is no reason for us to see God's words to Cain as
anything but an accurate foretelling of the kind of life Cain will
lead as a consequence of his sin.

Neither is there good reason to read Genesis 3:16 as a command to all women to be subject to their husbands' rule. Instead,
as in other passages that use the same language, we read God's
account of how things will be. *"Your desire shall be for your husband,
and he shall rule over you."*

If either God's words to Eve in 3:16 or to Adam in 3:17-19
were meant to be a command, and especially if they were meant to
be carried out by men and women under the New Covenant, there
should be a verse in the New Testament that instructs us so. Concerning the eating of herbs or vegetables, Romans 14:2 identifies
those who eat only vegetables as weak. Stronger believers who
believe they may eat all things are instructed not to judge those
who believe they may eat only herbs. The principle at stake is to
love one another, because, *"... the kingdom of God is not food and
drink, but righteousness and peace and joy in the Holy Spirit"* (14:17).

In her book, *Women Leaders and the Church*, Linda L. Belleville
points out there is no reference to Genesis 3:16 in the New Testament. In all instruction concerning the relationship between men
and women, while you can find reference to Adam's sin and Eve's
deception, *"a wife's desire for her husband and the husband's rule over
the wife (Gen. 3:16) are not cited even once"* (104).

If we want to know God's intent for men and women, we
need to look at the creation account before the fall. God made them,
male and female, in his image and told them to rule over the rest
of creation. It was a time of blessing and declaring the goodness of

creation. The only thing that was not good was for Adam to be alone. Even this, God made good again by taking woman out of man and allowing them to stand side by side. As soon as God completes the creation of one man and one woman, he invites them into the divine unity of marriage, declaring a man will be united to his wife and the two shall again be one flesh (Gen. 2:24).

Subordination of women appears after the Fall

The fall disrupts the divine oneness God desires. It changes the conditions of living on the earth. One of the changes, of course, is expressed in the relationship between men and women, specifically husbands and wives. The deterioration of Adam and Eve's relationship, in fact, appears to begin immediately. When God confronts Adam with his sin, Adam tries to shift the blame to Eve. Eve also shifted blame. She points to the serpent, and God responds by putting enmity between the accuser (Eve) and the accused (the serpent). This parallels the enmity that arose between men and women when Adam (the accuser) shifted blame to Eve (the accused). (See Mary Hayter, *The New Eve in Christ,* p. 107.)

The fact that the relationship between men and women deteriorated into one of dominant males and subordinate females does not mean this was God's will or desire. Compare Jesus' words in Matthew 19:8 where he said to the Pharisees, "*Moses, because of the hardness of your hearts, permitted you to divorce your wives, but from the beginning it was not so.*" The fact that men insisted on the right to divorce their wives and even managed to get Moses to give them a law to allow it, did not make divorce God's will or his desire. No more does the fact of the Fall and the deterioration of male/female relationships make the eternal subordination of women God's will or his desire.

In many countries, in many cultures, in many religions, in many sects of Christianity, men see themselves as primary and women as secondary. Roles of leadership and authority are presumed to be a part of the male domain. Women assume positions of dependence and subordination to men, some more willingly than others. The fact that it happens, the fact that later Scripture passages refer to it, does not prove it is God's will. If hardened hearts gave Israelite men the right to divorce their wives, couldn't hardened hearts perpetuate inequality between men and women, though "in the beginning, it was not so"?

I believe that in the beginning, God intended equal and uniquely individual men and women to be drawn together by a mutual attraction. He designed that they live and work together in a complimentary relationship and share the leadership and service to which they were called. Because of sin, however, the differences between men and women brought conflict and competition, and led to the perpetual subordination of women.

God told Eve her desire would be for her husband and he would rule over her. Today, some women desire to be ruled by their husbands. Admittedly, some women seek instead to rule over their husbands. Both extremes, to rule or be ruled, are a result of sin and the broken relationship between men and women that began at the fall. Both violate the oneness and unity God designed in creation.

As followers of God, I believe we should be aiming for a restoration of God's original desire and plan for the relationship between men and women. Instead, some believers seem to desire the perpetual consequences of sin, at least when it comes to the roles of men and women in the church and in the home.

Chapter~

4. The Maker of Adam and Eve

Around the time I was just beginning to wrap my mind around the idea of gender equality, I began looking closely at my own image of God. On an academic level, I knew God "transcended gender" and was neither male nor female. However, looking inward, I discovered my predominant imaginings of God were masculine.

One afternoon I went for a walk with my neighbor. It could be debated whether our walks were exercise for our bodies or simply a good excuse to talk. On this afternoon I decided to spice up our conversation with a provocative question. Playfully I halted my stride a bit, affected a pose, and said, "So! ... Is God a Man?"

A brief electric silence passed before she responded. With reddened face she cried, "Don't *go* there!"

Her response stunned me as much as my question must have done to her. The rest of our walk was a bit tense, as I tried to explain what motivated my question, and she tried to tell me how uncomfortable the whole subject made her feel.

We spend our lives trying to know God. Understanding who God is and how God participates in our lives occupies a good share of most people's lives, regardless of the language we use to describe it or the religious tradition that informs the search. Scriptures promise we will find God when we search with all our hearts (Jer. 29:13).

I was faced with the challenge of knowing God outside of, or beyond, my understanding of male and female. Obviously, it seemed, I was not going to explore the matter in casual conversations with other Christians. In my quiet prayer time I asked God to help me clarify my understanding of God outside the human limitation of sexuality. I was particularly grateful for the promise in James 1:5. Lacking wisdom, I knew I could ask God, and receive it generously and without reproach.

God Is Not a Man

Hosea 11: 9 "I am God and not man"

Though the Bible often speaks of God in male terms, calling God our Father and using the masculine pronoun (he, his, him), most Christians will acknowledge that God is neither male nor female. Though we recognize God created humankind with sexual differences, we also know God is far above humanity. Human sexuality is just that. Human. God transcends human sexuality, and the Scriptures carefully distance God from human sexuality for good reason.

I am so grateful to have encountered a book by Mary Hayter entitled *The New Eve in Christ* at this point in my study. In her discussion of God and gender, she points out that in ancient religions male gods were pro-creators who cavorted with female consorts as a source of life. The religion of the Bible offers stark contrast with the cavorting gods and goddesses in fertility rites and fertility cults. The nature religions of Israel's neighbors (i.e. the Canaanites) were preoccupied with fertility rites. Most ancient people who lived off the fruits of the land believed the fertility of the earth depended on divine sexual activity (Hayter, 14).

God intended Israel's religion would be markedly different from the other religions of the ancient world. Israel's God differed from local divinities. God's creation, for one thing, was not dependent on any Divine sexual act. There were no fertility rites. The God of Israel and of Christianity is not limited by a sexual identity.

Mary Hayter put it this way, "...one of the key factors which distinguished Israelite religion from other contemporary religions was the separation of sexuality from divine creation, that is the demythologizing of fertility" (17).

God forbids his people to associate him with other divine beings. God is "the absolute sovereign and omnipotent creator of the universe and its processes; he needed no female partner to perform the sex act with him and give birth to the earth and its inhabitants" (Hayter, 17).

One primary message of the Old Testament is this: God (meaning the Hebrew God, the one true God) is supernatural rather than natural, and transcends, or is far above creation. Theologians call this the denaturalization of God or the transcendence of God.

... God is supernatural rather than natural, and transcends, or is far above creation.

The Word says, *"For my thoughts are not your thoughts, neither are your ways my ways, saith the LORD. For as the heavens are higher than the earth, so are my ways higher than your ways, and my thoughts than your thoughts"* (Isa. 55:8-9).

God intended for us to know him as one apart from, and higher than ourselves. In John 4:24: Jesus put it this way, *God is spirit, and those who worship him must worship in spirit and truth.*

God is a Creator — not a pro-creator

The fatherhood of God is not to be understood in terms of sexuality or pro-creation. The father imagery in the Bible reflects God's person, his loving protection and authority, and **not** his maleness. Sound theology is not based on the assumption of a male God or deity. Both the conservative notion of a male God and the feminist protest of a female goddess misunderstand and misuse the Scriptures.

Even the imagery of Jesus as bridegroom requires understanding which points of comparison are valid. Conjugal imagery or the bridegroom image for God does not change the fact that God is fully outside human sexual differences.

I Believe in God the Father, but . . .

Joan Chittister, in her book *In Search of Belief*, looks closely at the words of the Apostle's Creed, taking each word or phrase to build a chapter. When she comes to "The Father," she dares to challenge the age-old tradition of the language of the creed. "The Father," she says, gives us a name and identity for God that presents limits to our understanding of who God is. With the best of intentions, the writers of the creed use the father image to denote God as our maker and as the one who cares for us like a loving father cares for his children. These are, of course, legitimate pictures of God's interaction with us, his creation.

Unfortunately, the church has relied more and more on "The Father" as a singular image for God, and in doing so, has created a false sense of God as a human male. The concept misses many biblical names and identities for God, some of which are feminine.

Jesus often relied on the Father as his title and image for God, even instructing us to pray, *"Our Father which art in heaven ..."* But he also softened his rebuke to the Pharisees by describing their relationship to God this way, *"O Jerusalem, Jerusalem, ... how often would I have gathered thy children together, even as a hen gathers her chickens under her wings, and ye would not!"* (Mat. 23:37). This is one of the feminine images the Scriptures use to help us better understand the nature of God and God's relationship to humankind.

In the gospels Jesus often called God "Father," a word translated from the Greek word "pater" which means father, generator, founder, male ancestor, or sometimes, both parents. Some Bible translations, like the New Revised Standard Version, translate the word pater as parents on more than one occasion (i.e. Hebrews 11:23 and 12:9). The King James Bible translates the word pater as father, except when it is used in the book of Hebrews to describe the actions of a parent or the parents of Moses.

Hebrews 11:23 says, "By faith Moses, when he was born, was hid three months of his parents (pater), because they saw he was a proper child; and they were not afraid of the King's commandment." Most modern English translations (including KJV, NKJ, NIV, RSV, NRSV, TLB, NLT, TNIV & NAS) translate "pater" as "parents" in this verse. Indeed, it would have created a conflict with other Scripture to translate this occurrence of pater as father. Exodus 2:2 records the event as follows: "And the woman conceived, and bare a son: and when she saw him that he was a goodly child, she hid him three months."

This one example at least demonstrates the possibility that the word we see as "Father" to describe God, could legitimately be translated as parent or even mother. Though I doubt any contemporary Bible translators would have the courage to translate it thus.

Admittedly, knowing God as Father helps us know God as our maker and as the one who cares for us like a loving father cares for his children. But knowing God as Father should not set limits around God, namely limiting the attributes of God to those of a human male.

No graven images

In Exodus 20:4 God commands this: *"Thou shalt not make unto thee any graven image, or any likeness of any thing that is in heaven above, or that is in the earth beneath. . ."* In Sunday School we all learned that God the Father did not want his people to worship idols. Perhaps it is time to look beyond the Sunday School understanding of God as Father and of the prohibition against making graven images to represent God. It may be time to see the larger concept God may have been trying to communicate.

Jeremiah 29:13 says, *"When you search for me, you will find me; if you seek me with all your heart."* Knowing God requires diligent seeking. We

... knowing God as Father helps us know God as our maker and as the one who cares for us like a loving father cares for his children.

... But knowing God as Father should not set limits around God, namely limiting the attributes of God to those of a human male.

can easily try to take a shortcut to knowing God by forming his likeness in our mind, comparing his likeness to things that are in heaven or things that are in earth. But the fact is, God is too big, too transcendent, too all-encompassing, to be contained in a single image, including the image of a human father.

To me, it's as if, in this prohibition against graven images, God is saying, "Do not fasten down your concept of me before I am fully known." He has promised that we will, one day, know the truth, and the truth will make us free. For now, I know I see through a glass darkly, but someday, I will see God face to face. I have come to believe that by trying to nail God's identity down to a single definable image, in this case, the image of a human male or father, we hinder our ability to truly know God. In fact, thinking that we already know God (or anything else, for that matter) can become our biggest barrier to knowing Him more fully.

Romans 1:19-20 is a verse that serves as a great motivator for missionaries to go to the remote regions of the world to proclaim the gospel. It says of the unrighteous, *"For what can be known about God is plain to them, because God has shown it to them. Ever since the creation of the world his invisible nature, namely, his eternal power and deity, has been clearly perceived in the things that have been made. So they are without excuse"* (Revised Standard Version).

It says God is clearly seen in the things that he has made. In other words, God is revealed in fathers and mothers and in sons and daughters, as well as in all created things. But God is not *contained* in these images. Merely revealed.

The unrighteous ones in Romans 1 are condemned because they knew God but failed to honor him as God. It says:

> *"Professing to be wise, they became fools, and exchanged the glory of the incorruptible God for an image in the form of corruptible man ..."(New American Standard).*

Has the church made a graven image of God as Father? Have Christians exchanged the glory of the incorruptible God for the image of a corruptible man? Have we, in our attempt to understand God, fixed our image of God on tablets of stone? Do we now bow ourselves before the graven image of a male God?"

Masculine and Feminine Imagery and Language

I now recognize some of the angst surrounding my question to my friend, "Is God a man?" It hinges on the language that teaches us about God. Not only is "Father" our primary image of God, our grammar has historically dictated the use of masculine pronouns (He, His, Him ...) to describe God.

However, the language that selects masculine images and pronouns cannot be used to defend the idea of a male God, any more than language or imagery proves a female God. The language that refers to God as father, for example, serves to help us understand some of the attributes of God. God is the source of our being, and our protector and provider.

In the introduction to her book, *Swallow's Nest*, Marchiene Vroon Rienstra speaks of one of the Old Testament names for God, El Shaddai "... which can be translated as 'breasted God,' since the root word in 'Shaddai' means 'female breast.' This is a clearly feminine name for God that supports the female images for God which are present in Scripture." God is the one who nurtures and nourishes us as mothers nurture and nourish their beloved children.

The Old Testament also includes several references to God that use other feminine imagery and language for God.

For example, God is described as a **seamstress** in Genesis 3:21; as a **midwife** in Psalms 22:9; as a **loving mother** in Isaiah 49:13-15, 66: 13 and in Psalms 131:2. God is said to be **in birth pangs** in Isaiah 42:14. God is called **both master and mistress** in Psalms 123: 2 (Hayter, 23). All of these images help us to see something about God which is more feminine than masculine.

This list of feminine images cannot be used to prove a female God any more than the abundant masculine images in Scripture can be used to prove a male God. Feminine images do, however, offer sufficient evidence that the nature of God encompasses both masculine and feminine attributes. The nature of God is reflected in both male and female, just as both male and female are created in the image of God.

If we are to truly know God, we will need to know him outside the boundaries of human sexuality. We will not need to invent a goddess to worship in place of God, but we will need to understand that using a masculine pronoun or image does not define God as a man. We might even learn to be comfortable thinking of God as mother, the one who nurtures us and cares for us with tenderness, the one whose wings overshadow us as a mother eagle protects the eaglets in her nest. We might see God as the midwife who brings us to new life as we are born again. Or even more powerful, I might see God as the one who suffered the birth pangs, the one who labored, who did the work and suffered the pain that I might enter the kingdom of God.

PART 2

Eve, As It Is Written

Chapter~

5. Daughters of Eve in the Old Testament

As conservative or evangelical Christians, we love to proclaim our everlasting allegiance to the Bible as God's inerrant Word to us, his church. There is, inherent in our claim, a note of pride and even judgment on those we deem less faithful to the Word of God. What we fail to recognize, I suspect, is the way we too have read the Bible selectively. We emphasize the details, stories and passages that enhance our way of thinking and reinforce or endorse our way of life. At the same time we tend to close our eyes to those passages that raise questions, confuse, or fail to endorse our fundamental belief system.

I'd like to share a good example of how such selectivity impacted the life of a good friend of mine. Rebecca grew up as a P.K. or Preacher's Kid. Her dad is a retired Baptist minister. Of course, Becky attended Sunday School week after week, and over a long enough period for the Bible stories in her primary classes to recycle more than once.

She especially remembers the story of "The Boy King Josiah" (2 Kings 21:24-23:34). This story seemed to be repeated often, always to emphasize this lesson: Even children can do great things for God. Even children can hear God and be obedient to his word. Even children can change the course of history by their faithfulness to God's call.

Several years after Rebecca grew to womanhood, after she graduated from Bethel College, married, and became the mother of two sons, she again encountered the story of "The Boy King Josiah." This time she was attending a class taught by the Rev.

Paul Howard entitled "Images of God." In one class Howard challenged his students with questions like these:

How often have you heard these images for God taught in church? God is like the house-cleaning wife who scours her floor looking for the coin that is lost? God is like the mother hen who gathers her chicks under the protection of her wings? For that matter, how often have you heard teachings about God's powerful women leaders like Huldah and Deborah?

Then he taught them the story of Huldah (2 Kings 22:14-20). When the boy king Josiah re-discovered the book of the law in the temple, he tore his robes and lamented God's wrath against his people for their disobedience. He told his high priest and assistants to go and inquire of the Lord. So they went to speak with Huldah, the prophetess. Huldah told them the Lord God would bring evil on this place. She prophesied the hard truth of the disaster God would send because of his anger against them for turning to other gods. However, she sent a word of mercy to the young King Josiah. Because of his humble and obedient heart toward God, the destruction would not come until he was safely gathered to his fathers, until he went to his grave in peace.

The word of the Lord came to the boy king through the courageous and prophetic voice of one of God's powerful women leaders. Upon hearing the word, the king chose his course of action. He destroyed all the idols and all of the alters to false gods. He restored Israel to the worship of her God.

My friend Rebecca was stunned. "Sure, the boy king found the book of the law, but what about the rest? What if he had never heard the Word of the Lord that came through Huldah, the wife of Shallum, who lived in Jerusalem in the second district?

"It seems to me," she said, recounting the story to me later, "Huldah's name is key to the story! And if Josiah provides a good model of ministry for Christian children, certainly this courageous and wise woman offers a model of ministry for both Christian women and children!"

Yet not once in all those retellings of the Sunday School version of the story had the name of Huldah been mentioned. And in case we are tempted to attribute such omission to the past, thinking we have become wiser in the present, Rebecca has one more story to tell.

"A few weeks ago," she told me, "my niece Emma just happened to bring me her Sunday School paper from that morning. The story was none other than 'The Boy King Josiah!' Had Emma heard anything about the woman who told the boy the word of the Lord? Was Huldah's name or mission even mentioned? No!

"I found myself getting all choked up, because the half truth of the Scriptures was still being perpetuated!

"I found myself getting all choked up," she said, "because the half truth of the Scriptures was still being perpetuated! It said to me that while we of evangelical background like to claim our lives are ruled by Scripture, that we owe our lives to its principles, it's not really true! We allow ourselves to be selective. We listen to some guys who, probably way back in the 50's, or 40's, decided which stories we would teach our children, and which ones we would omit because they portray roles not necessarily endorsed by the status quo!"

How much richer my own life could have been had only I heard the stories from God's Word that demonstrated even *girls* can do great things for God. Even girls can hear God and be obedient to the Word of God. Even girls can change the course of history by their faithfulness to God's call.

In this chapter we will look at biblical accounts to examine some of the roles and positions held by women in the Bible. Granted, we will be looking at women in a different culture than our own. We will be presuming, in most cases, God's approval of the roles women occupied in the time and culture in which these specific stories of the Bible were written. First let's take a brief look at how America culture has shaped male/female roles.

What do Happy Days have in common with the Bible?

If the 1950's model for the family is not the biblical model, what is?

Today's Christians often long for a return to the cultural values of earlier, presumably simpler, times. When it comes to the roles of women and men, in fact, many Christians would like to return to the "Happy Days" of the 1950's. They would feel much more comfortable with the roles assumed by men and women during that brief period of American history, when fathers provided the sole financial support for the family and mothers were not likely to work outside the home. It is presumed that moral decay and the feminism of the 1960's brought about an unfortunate shift away from this idealized standard for family life.

What we fail to recognize is that not only is this 1950's model for the family notably American, it also has little historical precedent. In other words, it existed for a brief period of history in America, but it did not exist before the 1950's. It is certainly very different than any cultural model found in the Bible.

In fact, in her book *Women Caught in the Conflict*, Rebecca Merril Groothuis says that the phenomenon of the 1950's American family came about as the result of a Victorian society altered by the Industrial Revolution. In Victorian culture, it was a matter of status for a man to possess a delicate flower of a wife who needed his protection. She was the opposite of her husband in every way, from her moral purity to her frailty. She was expected to be religious and sentimental, while he was expected to be rational and wise. Along came the Industrial Revolution, which began as early as 1790 in New England. Now in addition to the distorted picture of male and female roles provided by Victorian ideals, industry pulls the husband outside the home. His domain becomes the centers of industry, where all of the important primary work (productivity, financial gain) is done. The home, in his absence, becomes the domain of women and children and religion (Groothuis, 13-29).

We should also observe the effects of the Industrial revolution on single women. Many of those who worked in the factories—largely textile mills in New England—worked up to 70 hours a week for substandard wages. "Until the immigration wave of the 1840s, ... factory workers were single, white, native-born women recruited from middle-class New England farms" (from *Reader's Companion to U.S. Women's History*, Houghton Mifflin, on-line). Of course, position and pay varied according to a woman's race and class, but it was always substantially lower than that of her male co-workers.

This distorted Victorian model for the relationship between men and women was a far cry from anything we see in biblical accounts. In the culture of the Bible, the home was the center of commerce. Most often, the mother, father and children shared the labor that provided financial support for the family. This was true both in rural farming communities and in towns and villages.

In the rest of this chapter we will look at selected biblical examples of women and the roles they played in the history of Israel and the church. While not intended to be an exhaustive study, these observations should demonstrate that the biblical model of male-female relationships is nothing like the idealized period of American history preceding the feminism of the 1960's.

Old Testament Women

• Scripture does not support the Victorian idea of strong, invincible men and fragile, vulnerable women.

Deborah and Abigail

Deborah, a prophetess, was a judge in Israel (Judges 4 - 5). When she called up Barak and commanded him to march against the Canaanites, he refused to go unless she would go with him. She answered, *"Very well, I will go with you. But because of the way you are going about this, the honor will not be yours, for the Lord will hand Sisera over to a woman"* (4:9, NIV). Deborah is hardly a picture of a woman who needed the protection of a strong man in order to succeed.

• Nor do the women in the Bible demonstrate any inherent lack of intelligence or reasoning ability.

1 Samuel 25 tells us of "A certain man in . . . Carmel, (who) was very wealthy. His name was Nabal and his wife's name was **Abigail**. She was an intelligent and beautiful woman, but her husband . . . was surly and mean in his dealings" (2-3, NIV). And by the following story, we see he was also truly a fool. After David and his men had camped in the area surrounding Nabal's property, protecting his land and his herds, Nabal had the audacity to insult David, the anointed King of Israel, and refuse David's courteous request for provisions.

Fortunately, a servant "told Nabal's wife Abigail: 'David sent messengers from the desert to give our master his greetings, but he hurled insults at them. . .'" (14, NIV). And Abigail's quick thinking response saved her household from the swords of David's men. She loaded donkeys with abundant food, and hurried to David with her appeal on behalf of the men of her household. As a wise negotiator, she told David the benefit to himself if he could avoid unnecessary bloodshed.

David expressed his gratitude to Abigail:

"Praise be to the Lord, the God of Israel, who has sent you today to meet me. May you be blessed for your good judgment and for keeping me from bloodshed this day and from avenging myself with my own hands" (32-33, NIV).

He admits without Abigail's intervention not one man of her household would have been still alive at daybreak.

Proverbs 31

• Neither does Scripture support a view of the family that puts economic responsibility solely on the shoulders of the man. The wife of noble character so aptly described in Proverbs 31, in fact, contributes well to the economy of her household.

> *"Her husband has full confidence in her and lacks nothing of value" (11, NIV). "She rises up early to provide for her family and servants" (15).*

She possesses both good business sense and physical strength:

> *"She considers a field and buys it; out of her earnings she plants a vineyard ... her arms are strong for her tasks. She sees that her trading is profitable ... "(16-18, NIV) "She watches over the affairs of her household" (27, NIV).*

If Christians have any doubt whether the labors of a woman are worthy of at least equal pay to those of a man, we need only look to the scriptural injunction,

> *"Give her the reward she has earned, and let her works bring her praise at the city gate" (31, NIV).*

In our culture, employers still hesitate to follow this principle. One friend of mine, a single mom, worked for a large office furniture retailer in our area. She acquired a significant customer base by really zeroing in on her clients' needs and helping them plan effective work spaces. At her job performance review, she gently brought up the fact that her male counterparts earned a higher salary than she did. Based on her superior productivity, she requested a raise to bring her income in line with the other salesmen.

Thoughtlessly, her boss told her he paid the men more because they had families to support! He honestly thought he was somehow honoring God and the family by paying male heads of household more than he paid this female head of household! He probably felt he was honoring the Bible too, even though his practice opposed the scriptural mandate to give a faithful hardworking woman the reward she has earned.

Chapter~

6. Daughters of Eve in the New Testament

Now and then, as part of my spiritual practice, I read through old journals. It's a way of revisiting the journey God has brought me on thus far, a journey that includes a rebirth of understanding regarding males and females in the practice of Christianity. In April 1992, in my forties and not quite a year after earning my college degree, I wrote of taking risks. I recognized the risk of writing, even in my journal, my current thoughts and doubts about the gender issue:

> *"... even though it occupies a good deal of my thoughts*
> *lately. I find I read the Scriptures and listen to sermons with*
> *the gender question never far from my mind. You might say*
> *I am looking at the world through gender-colored glasses. If I*
> *were to try to put the gender question into words, it might*
> *read: 'What is God's heart toward women in the church and*
> *in the Kingdom of God? How do our traditions, teachings,*
> *prejudices, attitudes, and practices reflect or differ from*
> *God's heart toward women?"*

In the months, and even years that followed, I continued to explore my questions and record my experiences as they related to my identity, as a woman, in Christ. I approached some of the more difficult passages of Scripture and held them up to God for answers. I took courage in my reading outside of Scriptures, as God faithfully answered my gender question bit-by bit and day by day.

In April, 1996 I read a book by Madeleine L'Engle called *The Rock That Is Higher, Story as Truth.* In it she talks of confusing the very essence of truth by concentrating too hard on the facts. Scholars study the facts of Scripture and edit the life out of the story. Literalists tie themselves naively to the facts and lose the significance of the story. To believe the story, she reminds us, complete with virgin birth and miracles, requires childlike faith, while believing facts requires no faith at all (20-22).

I had no intention of disregarding the so called facts of Scripture, but taking in this nugget of wisdom about discerning truth in the stories God tells helped move me along in my search for God's heart toward women. In the same book, L' Engle speaks of the great reconciliation Jesus brought between male and female.

"Jesus broke all of the patriarchal rules" of His time and culture, she said. For example, He made friends with women. He did not hold the woman caught in adultery as the only responsible one and allow her to be stoned. He denounced the common practice of divorce (a man could simply write a letter of divorce and break covenant with his wife, and then take all her property). Jesus reconciled male and female, and it "terrified the religious leaders of the day" (28-29).

Indeed. It still terrifies them today.

Women in the Gospels

The New Testament testifies of women who made significant contributions to the cause of Christ. The gospels contain many stories of Jesus' interactions with women, most of which defied the societal norms that tended to disregard women. The rest of the New Testament includes women who helped to spread the gospel throughout the known world.

Women contributed to the economic needs of Jesus during the time of his ministry on earth. Jesus "went throughout every city and village, preaching . . . and the twelve were with him, And certain women, . . . Mary called Magdalene, out of whom went seven devils, And Joanna the wife of Chuza, Herod's steward, and Susanna, and many others, which ministered unto him of their substance" (Luke 8:1-3, KJV). The New International Version says, "These women were helping to support them out of their own means."

As Jesus lived out his life on earth, we see many examples of the great compassion he showed the women he encountered.

We all know the story of Mary and Martha, how Martha complained to Jesus that her sister Mary was not helping her with the household preparations, the cooking and serving required when offering hospitality and welcoming guests into her home. Jesus pointed out Martha's concern for many things, and gave Mary permission to choose something other than the traditional women's role of serving. Without being unkind to Martha for her choice of activity, he excused Mary from making the same choice. He honored her choice to sit at his feet and learn.

In a culture that generally excluded women from religious training, we find Mary seated at the feet of Jesus. Because of cultural differences, readers today may not recognize the significance of Mary's position. Seated at the feet of the master or teacher was a posture common for a rabbinical student.

In *Beyond the Curse*, Spencer states, "… to sit at someone's feet for a first century Jew (or other ancient person) would be an act to symbolize higher level formal education. Sitting at a rabbi's feet was a position typical of rabbinic students expressing respect to their rabbi" (58).

In the biblical account when Martha complained Mary was not helping with more traditional women's work, Jesus replied, *"but only one thing is needed. Mary has chosen what is better, and it will not be taken away from her"* (Luke 10:38-42).

Mary had chosen to sit at the feet of the Rabbi (John 1:38) in silence and submission. It was apparently not normal for her to do such a thing. It would have been *normal* for her to be helping Martha with the household duties, and serving the guests in the home.

By his action and his words, Jesus set aside the tradition that excluded women from learning and limited their sphere of influence to serving in the home.

Jesus gave Mary permission to excuse herself from traditional women's duties and take on a role her culture held as traditionally male. He not only allowed it, he honored her for her choice, saying she had chosen the better part.

Jesus disregards cultural norms which exclude and subjugate women

Jesus repeatedly disregarded the laws and traditions that governed attitudes and behavior toward women. On one occasion, to test Jesus and see if he would follow the law, the Pharisees brought to him a woman who had been caught in the act of adultery. They quoted the Scriptures to him: *"Now Moses in the law commanded us, that such should be stoned: but what sayest thou?"*

Most of us know the story. Jesus wrote with his finger on the ground. When they kept pressing him, he said, *"He that is without sin among you, let him first cast a stone at her,"* and her accusers left one by one.

We tell this story, but we fail to notice one thing. The Pharisees were right. The Scriptures – or the written law, did say the woman should be stoned. Jesus did not deny they were right. But he directed their minds to the spirit of the issue. Can you really condemn her based on the sin in your own life? Jesus did not invalidate the written law, but operated under a higher principle. And he called upon her accusers to do the same (John 8:3-11).

I wonder if today Jesus might be calling upon his church to operate under a higher principle toward women who were once caught eating the forbidden fruit. Is Jesus pleased when we say to him, *"The Scriptures say a woman should not usurp authority over a man and she should be silent and in subjection. What sayest thou?"*

Does he stoop down and write with his finger in the ground while we argue over who can and cannot hold leadership positions in the church? And when we press him enough, will he finally say, "Whichever one of you is willing to be the servant of all may take the first position of authority?"

There are many other examples of Jesus' compassion on women and his apparent lack of concern for traditions and laws. In Luke 13:12-16, Jesus sets a woman free from an infirmity that had kept her bent over for 18 years. The religious leaders were indignant because Jesus had done this service on the Sabbath day. Jesus responded by calling them hypocrites, or play-actors, phonies. Didn't they, after all, take their oxen and their donkeys out of their stalls for water on the Sabbath day? How much more did *"this woman, being a daughter of Abraham,"* deserve to be released from her bondage? The religious leaders had great zeal for the law, but when Jesus called them on their hypocrisy, verse 17 says, *"all his adversaries were ashamed, and all the people rejoiced."*

Even the Dogs

In Matthew 15:22-28, a Canaanite woman came to Jesus because she wanted healing for her daughter. Jesus at first refused, because, he said, his first mission was to the Jews. But the woman persisted and Jesus honored her faith with healing.

I have often wondered, if Jesus' first mission was to the house of Israel, at what point did his mission begin to change? I've heard the theology that God opened the gospel to the Gentiles because the Jews ultimately rejected Jesus. I can't help observing, however, that after the resurrection, Jews were actively preaching the gospel and receiving Christ. This was true at the time God brought Peter to the house of Cornelius (Acts 10) and also when God instructed Paul to preach to the Gentiles.

In Matthew 21, in order to rebuke the unbelieving Jewish leaders of the temple, Jesus told one parable to demonstrate how harlots and publicans would enter the kingdom of God before they did. After a second parable, he told them: *"The kingdom of God shall be taken from you, and given to a nation bringing forth the fruits thereof"* (43).

Jesus does, therefore, predict the change, and acknowledge the gospel will be given to the Gentile nations. He tells the Jewish leaders the *negative* consequences of their unbelief. But I believe this negative motivation is not God's only reason for extending grace to non-Jews.

Jesus expresses his favor on those non-Jews who respond to him with love and faith. After the Canaanite woman told Jesus that even the dogs eat the crumbs that fall from the master's table, Jesus answered her, *"Woman, great is your faith! Let it be done for you as you wish"* (15:28).

I believe God's *positive* motivation for extending the mission of Jesus beyond the nation of Israel could easily have begun with the faith of this woman.

In Mark 5:25-34, Jesus traveled with a leader in the synagogue, in response to the man's fervent request that Jesus heal his daughter. A large crowd thronged them as they went. A certain woman who had suffered from an issue of blood for 12 years, *"came in the press behind, and touched his garment."*

According to Jewish law and custom, any woman with an issue of blood was considered unclean. Any object or person who touched the unclean woman became unclean as well, and required ceremonial cleansing in order to be made clean again. It did not matter that this woman's bleeding continued for years on end. Leviticus 15:25 spells out the law for women who bled outside their normal menstrual cycle.

> *And if a woman have an issue of her blood many days out of the time of her separation, or if it run beyond the time of her*

*separation; all the days of the issue of her uncleanness shall
be as the days of her separation: she shall be unclean.*

This passage goes on to say that any man who touched either
the unclean woman or any of her things would also be unclean,
*"and shall wash his clothes, and bathe himself in water, and be unclean
until the evening."*

Jesus, in spite of the press of the crowd, knew immediately
someone had touched him. Most people who are familiar with the
story know how the disciples responded to Jesus when he asked,
"Who touched my clothes?" But how many of us can say for sure
how the woman herself responded to his demand to know who
touched him?

*"But the woman fearing and trembling, knowing what was
done in her, came and fell down before him, and told him all
the truth" (33).*

Why her fear and trembling? Could it be she feared both the
crowd and the man she had touched?

She knows healing has come into her body. To receive it, she
had boldly and intentionally pressed in with the crowd and she
had touched the rabbi, the healer. Had she not just violated the
law and made this miracle working man unclean by touching him?
Her very presence in the crowd violated her time of separation.
She would have been expected, in her condition, to remain isolated. Her society would have preferred she remain invisible.

Yet, even though verse 30 tells us Jesus immediately knew
"in himself that virtue had gone out of him" this Jewish rabbi does not
rebuke the woman for her violation of the law or for making him
unclean. Neither does he allow space or time for the people in the
crowd to condemn her actions.

He does, however, demand to know who touched him. All
hope of remaining anonymous is lost. In her fear and trembling,
knowing Jesus has healed her body, she speaks the truth to him.
He answers, out loud, for all the world to hear, *"Daughter, thy faith
hath made thee whole; go in peace, and be whole of thy plague."*

No condemnation. No anonymity. He grants her much more
than her good health. He grants her freedom from the law that has
bound her in isolation for many years. And he grants her visibility.
He does not require or allow her to remain invisible and unknown.
In a history that virtually ignores the actions and lives of women,
Jesus sees to it that her story is told.

This courageous woman's story is my story, and she tells it despite her issue of blood, her habit of isolation, her fear of the crowd and the man. Her story tried to stay buried, but when she reached out to touch the Savior, he would not let her story go untold.

... No condemnation.
No anonymity.

They devour widows' houses

When Jesus taught in the temple and warned about the hypocrisy of the scribes, he listed this among their sins: they *"devour widows' houses"* (Mark 12:40). As if to illustrate his point, he looked up and saw rich men casting their gifts into the temple treasury at the same time a certain widow put in her two mites. Her gift was greater than theirs, he explained, because hers was her whole livelihood, while their gift was more for show (41-44).

We need to see several verses together in context (Mark 12:38-13:2) to see how and why the temple leaders were devouring widow's houses. (Also read the account in Luke 20:46-21:5.)

It disturbed Jesus when religious leaders took advantage of poor widows, especially since the widows gave sacrificially and the temple leaders gave to keep up appearances. In the next verse (Mark 13:1) it says some spoke of the temple, *"how it was adorned with goodly stones and gifts."* Jesus tells them the day is soon coming when every stone will be torn down until not one stone is left upon another (13:2).

Now put it together. The temple treasury was being used for show, first by those who made a public show of putting in their gifts, and then by the temple leaders who used the funds to buy goodly stones and gifts. It all made the temple, and by the same token, its leaders, look good. What made this show diabolical to Jesus was the fact that the poor widows were innocently supporting this show with their very livelihood. The temple leaders carried on their show of pride and hypocrisy on the backs of poor widows. For this they incurred the condemnation of the Savior. (12:40).

Women in the rest of the New Testament

After Anna, the prophetess proclaimed the newborn Jesus to be the Messiah, (Luke 2:36-38) many women helped to spread the good news of Jesus to the world, both before and after the resurrection. It was a company of women who stayed with Jesus as he went to the cross (Matt. 27:55,56; Mark 15:40,41). The women were also the first to arrive at the tomb of Jesus early on the day after the Sabbath rest (Matthew 28:5-7; Mark 15:46,47; 16:1-6; Luke 23:55,56; 24:1-10). Christ first appeared as the risen Lord to Mary Magdalene (Mark 16:9, John 20: 14-18). In all four Gospel accounts of the resurrection, the women were the first witnesses of the resurrection and were sent to tell the disciples the good news.

Among the New Testament women who responded to the gospel was Lydia, a businesswoman, —"*a dealer in purple cloth,*"— and a worshiper of God. "*The Lord opened her heart to respond to Paul's message,*" Acts 16:14-15 says, and she and the members of her household were baptized. Then Lydia invited the apostle and his companions to come and stay at her house. "*And she persuaded us,*" the writer admits.

The apostle Paul acknowledged the important role of women in managing a home and raising children. In fact, in 1 Timothy 5:14, he instructs young widows to marry and rule their house: "*I will therefore that the younger women marry, bear children, guide the house...*" The Greek word translated 'guide the house" is 'oikodespoteo,' defined in Strong's dictionary as: (1) to be master (or head) of a house (2) to rule a household, manage family affairs." The Revised Standard Version says "rule their household" while other versions say "manage."

Paul often sends greetings to his friends Aquila and Priscilla, a couple who had traveled with him and had worked with him, both in making tents and in the work of the gospel. In Acts we learn Priscilla and Aquila heard the teaching of a man named Apollos. It turned out Apollos, though very fervent in his teaching, had not yet learned some of the basic doctrines of the church. He apparently did not know about baptism for believers, because it says he knew "*only the baptism of John.*" "*... And he began to speak boldly in the synagogue: whom when Aquila and Priscilla had heard, they took him unto them, and expounded unto him the way of God more perfectly*" (Acts 18:25-26). Note: many translations reverse the order of the names, for example, the NIV, RSV, and NAS say, "*...but when Priscilla and Aquila heard him, they ...*"

Apparently, both Priscilla and Aquila were instrumental in teaching Apollos the doctrines of God so he would be a more able minister. When Paul sends greetings to the church at Rome, he includes a greeting for his friends and fellow workers, Priscilla and Acquila (Romans 16:3). Paul often calls both men and women *'fellow laborers'* with him in the gospel. For example:

> "Yes, and I ask you, loyal yokefellow, help these
> women who have contended at my side in the cause of
> the gospel, along with Clement and the rest of my
> fellow workers, whose names are in the book of life"
> *(Phi. 4:3).*

Paul also greets Phoebe, who we know served the church in some capacity.

> *"I commend to you Phoebe our sister, who is a servant of the*
> *church in Cenchrea, that you may receive her in the Lord in*
> *a manner worthy of the saints, and assist her in whatever*
> *business she has need of you; for indeed she has been a*
> *helper of many and of myself also" (ROM 16:1-2, NIV).*

The word for servant in verse 1 is *diakonos*, a word that is translated variously as 'servant,' 'minister,' 'deacon,' and 'deaconess.' Paul often uses the term to describe himself as a minister of the gospel of Jesus Christ. He assigns the title to Apollos (1 Cor. 3:5), Tychicus (Col. 4:7), and Timothy (1 Thes. 3:2).

The word rendered 'helper' in the NIV is translated "succourer" in the King James. The Greek word is *prostatis,* which apparently means "a woman set over others; a female guardian, protectoress, patroness, caring for the affairs of others and aiding them with her resources." It comes from the word *proistemi* {pro-is'-tay-mee} meaning "to set or place before; to be over, to superintend, preside over; to be a protector or guardian (Strong's Dictionary in *Verse Search.* Bible Research Systems, 1999).

Of course there are many other scriptural examples of women playing significant roles in the establishment of the early church. I offer these few examples as a way of countering some extra-biblical notions of who and what women ought to be and do today as we strive to further God's kingdom on earth.

Chapter~

7. But the Scriptures Plainly Say. . .

Can we find alternative Interpretations for the Scriptures that seem to silence women in the Church?

My friend Mary, who now serves as the president of our local Christians for Biblical Equality chapter, tells her story this way. A few years ago she had finally worked up the courage to go to her pastor and discuss some of her concerns about the role of women in their church. By her observation women seemed to be excluded from most of the leadership positions. She said she'd like to see women taking a more active role in leading worship and making decisions.

Her pastor's simple response was this: "What part of the Bible did you want me to leave out?"

He was most likely referring to one of three New Testament passages that seem to exclude women from holding positions of authority in the church, as well as speaking or teaching. The passages I'm referring to are these: 1 Corinthians 11:3-16, 1 Corinthians 14:34-35, and 1 Timothy 2:11-15.

First the disclaimer:

I have often wished there was a way to write about the issue of equality between men and women without dealing with the three Bible passages that seemed to fly in the face of the principles I've come to accept. Virtually everything I know about these passages, I've learned by studying the works of real theologians and biblical scholars. I make no claim to being either. Neither will I attempt to present an exhaustive study of the biblical passages in question. Like so many Christians, when I set about to study this issue, I wanted to believe in the equality of men and women, and I also wanted to be true to the Scriptures. It was a great relief to me to find respected Christian scholars who supported legitimate alternative ways to look at these controversial passages.

In the next chapters, however, I do plan to address these three passages because, for readers who struggle with verses that seem to support the virtual silence of women in the church, I want to show that valid alternative readings of these passages do exist. The traditional interpretation is not the only one that will allow you to continue in faith toward God and love and honor for his Word. In fact, you may come to see, as I have, that relying on traditional interpretations of these passages causes serious contradictions with predominant, universal principles of Scripture.

For readers who are uncomfortable with any such re-evaluation of traditionally-held beliefs, I would like to caution you on two counts. Do not presume apostasy in those who look beyond the traditional views, and be careful your tradition does not become more important to you than the heart and will of God. (*"Making the word of God of no effect through your tradition which you have handed down,"* Mark 7:13 NKJ).

What does it mean to us today?

The statement entitled "Men, Women and Biblical Equality," published by Christians for Biblical Equality (CBE) has this to say about the passages in question: "… the few isolated texts that appear to restrict the full redemptive freedom of women must not be interpreted simplistically and in contradiction to the rest of Scripture, but their interpretation must take into account their relation to the broader teaching of Scripture and their total context."

In order to understand what the Bible says to us, we need to understand some basic principles of biblical interpretation. Of these, taking into account the broader teaching of Scripture is paramount. Principles I try to follow when interpreting Scripture are the ones set forth by Gordon D. Fee in his book, *Gospel and Spirit, Issues in New Testament Hermeneutics.* A quick summary follows:

In the world of biblical scholarship, interpreters are concerned with both exegesis and hermeneutics. In simplified terms, exegesis is the discovery of what the text meant originally and hermeneutics discovers what the text means to us now.

Three things are important in the discovery of what the text means:

First, look at the original setting. "The correct meaning of a passage must be something the author intended and the readers could have understood"(7).

Second, look for the Word of God in the original setting. What was God saying to the recipients about their particular situation?

And **third**, look for the Word of God for our situation.

Often we want to do this last step first. However, to understand what God truly wants to say to us today, the first two steps must not be bypassed. Since "very often the words of the epistles are culturally conditioned by the first century setting, if these words are going to be God's word to us, then we must first of all hear what God's word was to the original recipients" (8).

I know some people object to terms like culturally conditioned, cultural relevance, and historical particularity when it comes to interpreting Scripture. They want to say they take the whole Bible literally and strive to obey every word. Yet these same folks will read past a verse like Romans 16:16, *"Salute one another with a holy kiss,"* with hardly a thought.

There is little doubt as to what the passage means. Many newer translations say *"Greet one another with a holy kiss."* Most Christians I know greet one another with a handshake or a hearty hello. Sometimes good friends will even hug. Outside of romantic relationships, however, no one kisses.

Could we kiss one another? Certainly we could. Should we, in the light of the plain meaning of the text, suspend our traditions and change? We could, but we don't.

Here we have a passage of Scripture with clear meaning. We know what it says to do. We are perfectly able to do what it says. Yet, at least here in the West, we do not do it. And we know why.

Such instruction is obviously culturally conditioned. In some Middle Eastern countries you still see men greeting one another with a kiss. Most likely the same was true in the first century. Yet in our Western culture, a handshake is the more common symbol of greeting, while kissing is usually reserved for something more intimate.

We could interpret Paul's statement as a command to overcome our own cultural inhibition, abandon our customary handshakes, and replace them with kisses. We don't, because we know the statement has historical particularity and cultural relevance, whether or not we use those terms.

1 Timothy 5:23 says to stop drinking only water and drink some wine for your stomach's sake. (KJV: *Drink no longer water, but use a little wine for thy stomach's sake and thine often infirmities.*)

Here is another example of a verse most assume to have historical particularity. In other words, the writer addresses a particular person at a particular time and does not intend his instruction to be universally applied to all people at all times.

People of our time will decide whether or not to drink wine or strong drink based on a variety of factors. Most, however will decide without fear of disobedience to this biblical directive. A person who chooses to abstain from drinking wine (I'm not referring to grape juice, and neither is this passage) need not be concerned that he or she violates the biblical injunction to drink wine instead of water.

Perception is nine-tenths of understanding

Many things color the way we understand the Bible. It's easy to read familiar words expecting only confirmation of the things we have always believed or always been taught. Preconceptions are powerful. We see what we expect to see.

For the same reason, it is extremely difficult to proofread your own writing. Your mind can see missing words that you expected to be there. It's as if your brain is on auto-correct. Let's try a small experiment. Read the following familiar phrase:

"A bird in the the hand is worth two in the bush."

Did you read it correctly? Or did you fail to see the extra word? Looking again, you notice it reads "the the hand ..." Most people miss the extra "the" and read the phrase the way they *expect* it to be. Their minds auto-correct the phrase according to their predisposition.

The positive side to this quirk of human thinking is a little like the power of faith, which stands as *"the substance of things hoped for, the evidence of things not seen"* (Hebrews 11:1). For example, to the centurion who believed Jesus could heal his servant from a distance just by saying the word, Jesus said: *"Go thy way; and as thou hast believed, so be it done unto thee"* (Matthew 8:13).

Even secular science has begun to acknowledge the power of belief. Experiments in the field of quantum mechanics repeatedly demonstrate that what we **think** has the power to physically alter the things we observe. In the introduction to the book, *Taking the Quantum Leap, the New Physics for Non-Scientists* by Fred Alan Wolf, the concept is stated like this: "The gradual recognition that what we think may physically influence what we observe has led to a revolution in thought and philosophy, not to mention physics."

The point I am making is that our own perceptions can make us see things that are as though they are not, and things that are not as though they are. When interpreting the Bible, we must use caution lest we impose our own meaning on the text without adequately exploring the text and the context for the meaning God intended.

Christians and propaganda

Unfortunately, what we think is often influenced in one way or another by various forms of propaganda. Recently I attended a lecture by Randy Bytwerk, professor in the department of Communication Arts and Sciences at Calvin College and an expert on propaganda. He described the main elements of propaganda as "over simplification and demonization."

Conflicting opinions and the need to emphasize a point often lead speakers and writers to employ these elements. Arguing couples, for example, employ phrases like *"you always ..."* or *"you never ...,"* even though the resulting accusation is seldom technically accurate. It oversimplifies the situation and demonizes the other person.

Here's a phrase I often hear in Christian gatherings: "God said it, I believe it, and that settles it." I've said this one myself once or twice. Yet it certainly is an oversimplification. And what about this one, "We just believe the Bible and do what it says?"

The church has been struggling for two thousand years over what the Bible says and what it means. Besides being simplistic, such a statement often stands as an accusation against everyone else. The implication is, "If I agree with God, and you disagree with me, then you, by inference, disagree with God. I am good for I have aligned myself with God, and he and I stand together to defend the truth." You, of course, are the bad guy.

Since propaganda paints everything as black and white, under its umbrella the people who agree with me are the good guys whose ideas are all good and true. Those who disagree are bad guys with false ideas. A great gulf is fixed between opposing ideas, and anyone who ventures into the gulf (the place where honest questions are asked) will be accused of compromising the truth and making alliance with the enemy.

In most cases, however, the line between good and evil, right and wrong, is not so easily discerned. And in the case of Christians who disagree over the interpretation of the Bible, it requires some serious propaganda to make those Christians with variant positions into the bad people with the bad ideas.

When I see Christian leaders resorting to propaganda, name calling or demonizing the opposition and oversimplifying the opposing point of view, (I wish I could say I don't see it very often) I see it as a warning. It's a red flag that makes me suspicious of the ideas and motivation of the accusers. It makes me want to look long and hard at the ideas that precipitate such reactionary and dishonest behavior, and prejudices me toward the ideas of the one so accused. Since the Bible so clearly tells us to speak the truth in love, to love our enemies and to pray for those who spitefully use us, it's hard to see how someone who claims to defend the Bible can so mistreat their brothers and sisters in Christ.

For a recent example, you need only to have listened in on the controversy surrounding the decision by the International Bible Society and Zondervan Publishing House (Grand Rapids, MI) to release *Today's New International Version.* You would have heard opponents to the new translation oversimplify and even change the clearly defined goals of the IBS, using loaded terms like "gender neutral version" and "feminist effort to re-engineer society." You would have heard some Christians demonize those whose stated goal was "to produce a Bible easily understood by modern readers but still faithful to its original meaning." To hear opponents tell it, what they **really** wanted was to "abandon God's parameters for the home and for the church." ("Critics speak out against Today's New International Version," *The Grand Rapids Press*, Feb. 02, 2002).

Controversies over interpretation of Scripture are certainly nothing new to the practice of faith. The New Testament itself contains accounts of early controversies between Christian leaders.

A major dispute arose over the issue of circumcision

In the first century church, Jewish Christians continued to worship in the temple and did not abandon Jewish religious practices. When non-Jews became part of the new community of believers, however, Paul emphatically denied non-Jewish believers should be subject to Jewish laws.

> *But some of the sect of the Pharisees who believed rose up,*
> *saying, "It is necessary to circumcise them, and to command*
> *them to keep the law of Moses." So the apostles and elders*
> *came together to consider this matter (Acts 15:5-6 NKJ).*

Keep in mind, the Jewish Christians who wanted Gentile believers to be circumcised were doing their best to obey the Scriptures. The Word of God as they knew it proclaimed, "*And ye shall circumcise the flesh of your foreskin; and it shall be a token of the covenant between me and you*" (Gen. 17:11). Before this controversy heated up, what reason would they have had to think circumcision was no longer required? The issue did not even come up until after Paul began preaching the gospel to the Gentiles.

The Holy Spirit, through Paul, revealed that in Christ we are under a new covenant, a covenant of grace instead of a covenant of law. Inclusive by design, the new covenant makes us all one in Christ, whether Jew, Greek, male, female, slave or free (Gal. 3:28).

The old sign, like the covenant it stood for, was exclusive. To receive the sign, you had to be Jewish and you had to be male. Circumcision could not remain as the sign of the New Covenant because it is both gender and racially exclusive.

Under the Old Covenant, those who **were far away** (Eph. 2:13) were **excluded** from the covenant, which was sealed through the circumcision of male Jewish followers. Under the New Covenant, Jew or Gentile no longer matters; Slave or free no longer matters; Male or female no longer matters. The blood of the Old Covenant, whether the blood of circumcision or sacrifice, was only a sign of redemption to come. The blood of the New Covenant belongs to our Savior, the Lamb of God. His blood, not ours, seals our promise, making circumcision and the sacrifice of animals obsolete.

Paul took the radical position, circumcision is not required under the New Covenant. At one point, he also said, "*Mark my words! I, Paul, tell you that if you let yourselves be circumcised, Christ will be of no value to you at all*" (Galatians 5:2 NIV). Now to emphasize the point, the next verse says, "*Again I declare to every man who lets himself be circumcised that he is obligated to obey the whole law.*"

No New Testament law was established

At first glance, it might appear Paul was establishing a new law for them. Instead of required, circumcision was now forbidden. But it was Paul who said,

> *"All things are lawful unto me, but all things are not*
> *expedient. All things are lawful for me, but I will not be*
> *brought under the power of any" (1 Cor. 6:12).*

Paul's actions prove his words true. In Acts 16 Paul meets a young disciple named Timothy who had a believing Jewish mother and a Greek father. Verse 3 says,

> *Paul wanted to take him along on the journey, so he*
> *circumcised him because of the Jews who lived there, for they*
> *all knew his father was a Greek" (NIV).*

Paul was not brought under the power of even his own words concerning circumcision, because another important principle was at stake. Under the New Covenant, we (the church) are not under the law. All things are lawful for us. We are free to decide what things are expedient and what things are not. In Timothy's case, Paul felt it was expedient for the young man to be circumcised.

Being under grace and not under the law is sometimes a hard concept for believers to grasp. We are sometimes more comfortable making rules and living under their security than living as freeborn sons of God. (We are joint heirs with Jesus, no longer children who must remain under the guardianship of the law. See Gal. 4:1-7)

It's easy to fall into the trap of thinking we can work to earn favor with God. But Paul reminds us, *"And if by grace, then it is no longer by works; if it were, grace would no longer be grace"* (Romans 11:6). As a church, we need to be on guard against the temptation to create a New Testament Law, and substitute our law for the grace that is ours in Christ Jesus.

Chapter~

8. As Christ Is The Head Of The Church

Regarding head coverings, metaphors and being the glory of God

1 Corinthians 11:3-16

But I would have you know, that the head of every man is Christ; and the head of the woman is the man; and the head of Christ is God ... (11:3).

It is with a certain dread I enter this passage of Scripture into the arguments for equality (not sameness) among women and men in the church of Jesus Christ. I can already hear the "Ah-hah!" my admission may elicit from believers in divinely assigned gender roles. It's just this. Even as I have come to new understanding about the unity and oneness of believers in Christ, even as I have thanked God for continuing to show me his heart toward women, I have still struggled with what appears to be the obvious meaning in this passage. Especially when I try to rely totally on my first impression of the meaning of the words.

I know Christians who believe the meaning of the Bible should be plain to any and all readers, or at least to all believing readers. They are suspicious of any attempt to look beyond the obvious meaning of the text, especially when the obvious meaning clearly backs up a traditional or personal belief.

From the time I first began my study, I have sensed others questioning my motives for looking beyond the obvious meaning of passages like I Corinthians 11. During one of those seasons when I found myself seriously questioning my own motives, I remembered the passage in which Paul condemns those who oppose him on the issue of circumcision. He says if they are so insistent that Gentile believers be circumcised, they should *"...go the whole way and emasculate themselves!"* (Gal.5:12, NIV).

The translators of the King James Version –most likely male translators—may have been a bit reluctant to translate these words clearly or literally. They chose these words: *"I would they were even cut off which trouble you."*

Before reading other translations, I interpreted Paul's meaning as hoping they were cut off from fellowship! Perhaps if the King's scribes or translators had been women, they would not have been so hesitant to use words that clearly reflected the author's meaning.

The perspective helped me to accept my motivation to look again at the so called obvious meanings of three New Testament Scripture passages most often quoted by those who would keep women from equal participation in their faith. The passages again are: 1 Corinthians 11:3-16, 1 Corinthians 14:34-35, and 1 Timothy 2:11-15, the subject of this and the next two chapters respectively.

My faith in two particular scriptures has helped me continue with these next three chapters. One is the verse in James 1:5, the one that promises wisdom to all who ask. The second is the one in Acts about the people from Berea who are honored for their careful searching of the Scriptures:

> *These (people from Berea) were more noble than those in Thessalonica, in that they received the word with all readiness of mind, and searched the Scriptures daily, whether those things were so (Acts 17:11).*

One of the chief texts traditionalists use to prove their position is 1 Corinthians 11:3-16. This is the passage in which Paul exhorts the Corinthians about head coverings, letting them know it is proper for women, and not men, to have their heads covered during public worship services. He was evidently concerned that improper attire could bring dishonor to the message of the gospel. To buffer his case he draws a parallel, or a word play if you will, between the proper head covering and the place of Christ as head of the church.

> *But I would have you know, that the head of every man is Christ; and the head of the woman is the man; and the head of Christ is God (11:3)*

To the traditionalist this verse sets up a chain of command. It's not hard to see how they come to their conclusions. All it takes is a slight rearrangement of the words and borrowing a modern English figurative meaning for the word *head*.

The case for a chain of command would be easier to make if the words were arranged like this: *God is the head of Christ, Christ is the head of the man, and the man is the head of the woman.* Then all you would have to do is assume the word *head* is used to mean chief or boss, the way we use it in modern English.

I would like us to be "more noble," like the people from Berea, who received the word with readiness of mind and searched the Scriptures to see if it was so.

> *... All it takes is a slight re-arrangement of the words and borrowing a modern English figurative meaning for the word* head.

Does "head" mean leader? Or source?

Part of the difficulty understanding this passage centers on our understanding of the word *head*. The Greek word for *head* is *kephale*. In most places the word is used, it simply means the literal head, as in the one that sits on your shoulders. In several places in Scripture, however, the word is used as a metaphor, giving a figurative meaning to the literal word for the body part.

Jesus used the word figuratively when he called himself the "head of the corner" as in the first cornerstone of a building. (*And have ye not read this scripture; The stone which the builders rejected is become the head of the corner?* Mark 12:10). Here the word head is not used as a metaphor to mean ruler, or leader. Here the meaning is more like the head of a river, as in the beginning or source. The head of the corner or cornerstone is the foundation stone, the first one, the one upon which all the other stones will be built.

> *For the husband is the head of the wife, even as Christ is the head of the church: and he is the savior of the body. Eph. 5:23*

When the word is used as a picture of relationships between men and women or husbands and wives, as it is in Ephesians 5:23, our task is to discover what the picture or metaphor implies. We should not merely assume we know because of the way the word is most often used in today's language. It's too important for such assumptions, because, after all, *"the husband is the head of the wife, even as Christ is the head of the church."*

If we misunderstand the relationship between men and women or husbands and wives, we will also misunderstand the relationship between Christ and the church. It is imperative that we understand what it means to be "the head of."

Here in Ephesians, as in 1 Corinthians 11:3, the word head is used figuratively. Unfortunately, modern English has given us a strong impression about the figurative meaning of head. Today when we hear about the head of something or someone, we think leader or head honcho.

One thing we must observe. In contrast to the first century, we in this century have a far different understanding about the function of our head in relation to the rest of our body. Because of scientific discoveries, we now know our mind and emotions are products of our brain, not our heart, as people once believed.

Our head has taken on new significance to us since our understanding of physiology has increased. We understand the brain, and therefore the head, is the control center of the body. Therefore, it is not unusual for modern readers to assume if Paul says Christ is the head of the church and a man is the head of his wife, he must mean Christ is chief controller of the church, and a man must be the chief controller of his wife.

However, in order to understand these relationships as Paul intended us to understand them, we need to understand more than "How is the head related to the body?" We need to know how Paul and his first century audience would have perceived the relationship between the head and the body.

As the previous paragraphs implied, to the first century audience the **heart** was the control center of the body, the place of thoughts and ideas and of innermost being. The **head**, in contrast, was **the source of life**. After all, if you wanted to kill someone, you cut off his head. (For an extensive discussion on the metaphorical meaning of head in Greek language and literature, see Gordon Fee's commentary on 1 Corinthians, pages 502-504, including notes. He concludes that a better understanding of the symbolic use of "head" would be as the "source" as in "source of life." Also, Gilbert

Bilezikian's book *Beyond Sex Roles* contains a thorough discussion of the New Testament meaning of "head."

Our own language and culture is not devoid of this understanding of the word head. Have you ever heard the expression, "She's running around like a chicken with her head cut off?" I'll bet you never once thought the saying meant the chicken had been cut off from her boss! The poor cluck has lost her source of life, her window to the world, but not her connection to the authority over her life.

The idea that head means source of life seems to be confirmed in verses 8 and 9, *"For man did not come from woman, but woman from man; neither was man created for woman, but woman for man"* Originally, according to the Genesis account, man was the source of woman who was taken from the man.

As in First Timothy 2, Paul is making reference to Adam and Eve. Adam was formed first, and Eve was formed from him and for him. So Adam is the source of Eve. Paul goes on to point out that she is his glory, and without her, he is incomplete. None-the-less, as her source he is worthy of honor.

Her appearance during worship

By reminding these women of the honor they owe to the men who were their original source of life, Paul takes issue with their appearance during worship. By their appearance (without a head covering, whether it refers to a bald head, short hair instead of long, or to not wearing a veil, we are not certain), he says, they are dishonoring the relationship between themselves and the men.

Dishonoring the relationship with an uncovered head brings shame on the "head," or source (here the author uses a play on words to illustrate his point). Paul's underlying concern, consistent with all we know of Paul, is that this shame will reflect poorly on the gospel of Christ.

As mentioned earlier, to interpret head as authority or ruler, we face the temptation to rearrange the text in order to make it more logical. It would follow a more logical progression, in this case, for the passage to say: *a. God is the authority over Christ and b. Christ is the authority over man and c. man is the authority over woman.*

Just to remind you, the passage reads: *"the head of every man is Christ; and the head of the woman is the man; and the head of Christ is God."*

Two things are wrong with the interpretation that assigns the meaning of ruler or chief to the word head. One, of course, is the unreasonableness of rearranging a scriptural text to make it fit better with our expected meaning. Better that we look carefully at the order as it does appear, and try to understand the meaning implied by the order the author chose.

The other has to do with a basic Christian understanding of God and the Trinity. The interpretation of head as chief authority implies a hierarchy within the persons of the God-head. While some modern scholars and theologians do seem to advocate an interpretation of Scripture which allows for ranking Father, Son and Holy Spirit with differing levels of authority (mostly in defense of their traditional understanding of male/female relationships), historical Christian theology stresses instead the oneness and equality of the three persons of the Trinity.

Gilbert Bilezikian offers a thorough discussion of this theological principle in his essay, "Hermeneutical Bungee-Jumping: Subordination in the Godhead," and in his book *Community 101*. I will simply offer his quote from the doctrinal statement of the Evangelical Theological Society:

> *God is a Trinity, Father, Son, and Holy Spirit, each an uncreated person, one in essence, equal in power and glory"*
> *(from Community 101, page 18).*

In order to interpret the head metaphor to mean chief or authority, we are forced to change an important foundational doctrine of Christianity, a doctrine that defines the oneness and equality of the Father, Son and Holy Spirit.

However, by understanding head in the way Paul and his first century audience were likely to understand it, we solve these two difficulties with the text. By accepting that the better meaning for head is source, we consequently have no more need to rearrange the order of Paul's words in 11:3. Neither do we need to change a long held doctrine of the Trinity that grants equality to the persons of the Godhead.

> *But I would have you know, that the head* (source) *of every man is Christ; and the head* (source) *of the woman is the man; and the head* (source) *of Christ is God.*

It makes perfect sense in this order. Just as Christ is the source of every man (according to John 1:3, all things were made by him), the man is the source of the woman (she was taken out of man,

Genesis 2:23), and God is the source of Christ (His only begotten son, John 3:16).

Paul here reminds the members of the Corinthian church that Adam was created first and the woman came from the man. As the source of the female, the male is worthy of honor. In the culture of the Corinthian church, Paul felt this honor required that women wear head coverings.

Christ as the Source

For your further consideration, please note than when Paul calls Christ the head of the church in Col. 1:18, the context implies Christ is the source of its being:

> *"He is the image of the invisible God, the firstborn over* (or source of) *all creation. For by him all things were created: things in heaven and on earth, visible and invisible, whether thrones or powers or rulers or authorities; all things were created by him and for him. He is before all things, and in him all things hold together. And he is the head of the body, the church . . . (Col. 1:15-18).*

Paul's words are consistent with the gospel of John 1:1—4:

> *"In the beginning was the Word, and the Word was with God, and the Word was God. The same was in the beginning with God. All things were made by him; and without him was not any thing made that was made. In him was life; and the life was the light of men.*

Authority is mentioned in this verse, but only to say that Christ created even the rulers and the authorities. He is the source of thrones and powers because he is the source of all things in heaven and earth. Christ is the firstborn over all creation. He came first. *He is before all things.* He is the source of all things, and he is the source of the body, the church.

The imagery of Christ as head meaning source of life, and source of the body of Christ, shows up again in Ephesians 4:15-16:

> *... but, speaking the truth in love, may grow up in all things into Him who is the head - Christ - from whom the whole body, joined and knit together by what every joint supplies, ... working by which every part does its share, causes growth of the body for the edifying of itself in love.*

This time the head, Christ, is the source from which the whole body is joined together, and our joining to the source causes us to grow and be edified. Just like Jesus calls himself the vine, and we who follow him the branches, we are meant to see our connection first to our source, and then to one another in the body of Christ.

First has always been a place of honor among people. We honor the firstborn child or grandchild. We honor the first to run a mile in a minute, even though many have done it since. We honor the first explorers to set foot on our soil, and the first to declare our independence from foreign control in order to birth our nation. George Washington was one of many presidential leaders of our nation, but we give him special honor because he was first.

We have no difficulty honoring Christ as the leader and chief controller of the church. But the verses that call him *head* of the church are telling us something more, something wonderful beyond what we already assume.

Jesus is our first. We honor him as first cornerstone of the church, as firstborn among us. Without Jesus as first, as source, we cannot be, either as individuals or as his corporate body. We are his body; he is our head. We are the church. He is the first cornerstone on which the church is built. He is the firstborn among us. We come after him, and he has made us joint heirs with him.

In 1 Corinthians 11, Paul draws a parallel between Christ, who came first, and Adam, who arrived first on the scene in Genesis 1. Ephesians 5:23 draws the parallel between a husband and his wife and Christ and his church. It says, *"For the husband is the head of the wife, even as Christ is the head of the church: and he is the savior of the body."*

The rest of the passage goes on to show how Christ is the model for the husband's role in his relationship to his wife. Rebecca Merrill Groothuis in *Good News for Women* says, "The husband's role is described here as life-giving, self-giving love, which is analogous to the role of Christ as Savior of his body, the church."

She goes on to say we must observe carefully what the comparison does and does not say about husbands and wives. For example, this passage does not mention "either the authority of the husband over his wife (which he had through civil law at the time of Paul's writing) or the authority of Christ over the church (which he has always had in full measure)."

As head, the husband loves and serves his wife as he cares for and serves his own body, just as Christ does for the church. Remember, the relationship of head to body, in the understanding of a first century reader, is a relationship of source, as in the source of life. If you remove the head from the body, the body cannot live. For that matter, neither can the head. It is this interdependence that Paul brings us back to in 1 Corinthians 11:11-12:

> *Nevertheless neither is the man without the woman, neither the woman without the man, in the Lord. For as the woman is of the man, even so is the man also by the woman; but all things of God.*

Paul could have easily used this place to reinforce a hierarchy of authority between men and women, if indeed that was what he had been trying to say. He did not, and I believe he offers these verses to guard against any such wrong assumptions.

She ought to have power on her head

The only time the word "authority" does appear in verse 10, it refers to the woman's own authority. *"For this reason,* (because woman was made from and for man, verses 8-9) *ought the woman to have power* (*exousia*, authority) *on her head because of the angels."*

Given the construction and context of the sentence, *"the woman should have authority"* means, like in all other uses of the word *exousia*, the woman has or possesses (her own) authority. It does not mean someone else (i.e. a man) possesses or exercises authority over her (Fee's commentary on 1 Corinthians, p.520).

"On her head" may suggest she should have the authority to decide whether or not to cover her head.

Because of the angels

"Because of the angels" has been interpreted many ways. For example, since in 6:3, Paul says the saints will judge angels, one explanation says, since someday these same women will judge angels, they ought to be able to exercise enough authority to decide whether or not to cover their heads during worship services. Some other scholars have said it was because women were already speaking the language of angels (13:1). (See Gordon D. Fee's commentary on 1 Corinthians, p. 518-522).

In my own research, I found verse 10 cross-referenced to Ecc. 5:6, which gives specific instructions about making and keeping vows. It warns against making a vow and then claiming it was a mistake. *"And do not protest to the temple messenger [NIV], -or- nei-*

ther say thou before the angel [KJV] 'My vow was a mistake.'" Apparently, to the ancient Jew, the angels were witnesses of vows made and kept.

From earlier research, I know in the Old Testament neither a married woman nor an unmarried daughter could vow her own vow. Numbers 30:3-16 gives instructions to both husbands and to fathers on how to nullify any vow made by a wife or a daughter. Verse 13: *"Her husband may confirm or nullify any vow she makes or any sworn pledge to deny herself."*

Paul could be saying this: Since under the New Covenant, a woman (or wife) is free to vow her own vow, including the marriage vow, she should show proper respect for her relationship to the men in the church (or to her husband) by keeping her head covered, because of the angels who stand as witness to her vow.

She brings him glory

Before I can move on to the next passage, I want share with you the prayer I prayed after a startling encounter with verse 7, which says, *"...since he (man) is the image and glory of God; but the woman is the glory of man."*

> *What do I do with this one, Lord? This verse, like a few others I've encounter in your word, seems to contradict the things you are showing me about your heart towards women. Will you show me what is right? Will you help me to understand what the author meant and what you are saying to us in this verse?*

This is like the prayer I've prayed over and over again when I confront some of the more difficult passages concerning the role of women in the church and family. And many times God has led me to other people, scholars and authors who have wrestled before me with the same issues.

For this verse I again found what I was looking for in the writings of Gilbert Bilezikian and Gordon Fee.

On page 22 of his book, *Community 101,* Bilezikian makes this statement: "Scripture affirms the full participation of both man and woman in the image of God." He shows how this is demonstrated first in the Genesis account, then confirmed in 1 Corinthians 11:7-9. His explanation lends understanding to Paul's intent in the Corinthian passage:

Because originally, man did not come from woman but from God, he reflects the image and glory of God. Because the woman came from the man and was created for man as his helper-rescuer, she obviously shares in that divine image and glory by virtue of her derivation; however, in addition, she also reflects the glory of man from whom she was taken.

Let me paraphrase: Man came directly from God and therefore he reflects the image and glory of God. Woman comes from man. She is no less a reflection of the image and glory of God, but because she came from man and was created for him, she also reflects the glory of man.

In his commentary on I Corinthians, Gordon Fee concurs. Paul is not saying only males are made in God's image. He uses the word glory, which does not occur in the creation account. He says a woman is the glory of her husband the way a man is the glory of God. The most likely definition of glory, he says, is: "The existence of one brings honor and glory to the other." (516). Therefore, the existence of man brings glory to God, and the existence of woman brings glory to man as well as to God. Both are true, and they are not mutually exclusive.

In other words, Paul is **not** saying the existence of woman brings glory to man **instead of** to God. Paul is merely pointing out how a woman is related to a man as his glory. With a prayer of thanksgiving, I am able to rest.

Regarding relationships, respect and relative authority

According to Fee, the gist of 1 Corinthians 11:3-16 is this: The women in the Corinthian church, by their appearance — namely by what they are not wearing on their head— are breaking down the distinction between men and women, and thus disregarding the proper relationship between men and women. He emphasizes the need for women to respect the relationship by reminding them, women were created **from** the man and **for** the man, and not the other way around.

In other words: "women, you are here because Adam was your source of life. You are his glory, because you were created from him and for his sake. Both of you reflect the image and glory of God."

Paul does not, however, attempt to establish any hierarchy of authority between men and women. In fact, in verses 11 and 12, he seems to be guarding against just such an assumption.

"In the Lord, however, woman is not independent of man, nor is man independent of woman. For as woman came from man, so also man is born of woman. But everything comes from God" (NIV).

Paul seems to be aware verses 8 and 9 could be wrongly construed to indicate woman's subordination to man. Conversely, a woman could wrongly use her new-found authority (verse 10). Verses 11 and 12 seem designed to limit the application of verses 8-10 (see Fee, 523).

Yes, she was made for his sake, but she does not exist for his purposes, to be subject to his whims and will. Yes, she has authority over her own self, but she should not forget from whence she came. Just as she now has power to give birth to a man, she should remember that man, through Adam, gave life to her. God has arranged things so in the Lord, one cannot exist without the other. According to God's design, men and women are mutually dependent on one another.

Don't pour new wine into old wineskins

Many Christians truly believe the Bible says women should not have authority over a man. We will deal specifically with that passage soon enough, but for now, let us assume, for the sake of argument, God has given men authority over women, or at least has given husbands authority over wives.

Jesus said, *"All authority has been given to Me in heaven and on earth"* (Matt. 28:18). And with this authority, he commissioned his disciples to go into all the world and make disciples. In Mark he told them a parable which began, *"For the Son of Man is as a man taking a far journey, who left his house, and gave authority to his servants,"* (Mark 13:34).

Jesus said he has been given all authority. He in turn gives his authority to his servants. With Jesus as our model, even if we assume for a moment the servants who received his authority were men, how should we expect those servants to handle their new found authority?

When it comes to husbands and wives, Paul clearly teaches that husbands are to follow Christ's example. *Husbands, love your wives, just as Christ loved the church and gave himself up for her* (Eph. 5:25). Christ set this example for us, and he only did what he saw the Father doing (John 5:19). The Father had given all his authority to the Son. The Son was under no obligation to share his authority with his servants, but it appears, just as freely as he laid down his life for us, he freely gave us his authority.

Following Christ's example, can you see any reason the servants of Jesus should choose to hoard his authority for themselves, rather than freely share it with slaves or Greeks or women?

The twelve disciples may have been a small contingency of Jewish men, but the evidence of Scripture testifies Christ's power and authority did not remain exclusively in the male Jewish camp. He told his disciples to wait in Jerusalem for the promise of the Holy Spirit, so they would be empowered to go into all the world, to every nation, and make disciples.

> *"But ye shall receive power, after the Holy Ghost is come upon you: and ye shall be witnesses unto me* . . . (Acts 1:8).

Acts 1 also says about 120 disciples were assembled in Jerusalem, a number which included both men and women (13-15). And when the promise came, we know the Holy Spirit did not fall only on the eleven, nor did he fall only on the men. The words of the prophet Joel were fulfilled,

> *"And it shall come to pass in the last days, saith God, I will pour out of my Spirit upon all flesh: and your sons and your daughters shall prophesy, and your young men shall see visions, and your old men shall dream dreams: And on my servants and on my handmaidens I will pour out in those days of my Spirit; and they shall prophesy" (Acts 2:17-18).*

God's plan and purpose was to give his power and authority to his people, so his people could go into all the world, to every tribe and nation, and make disciples, bringing men and women into his kingdom. With a great army of Spirit empowered believers, the potential for spreading the gospel should be great. Did God intend to limit the power of over half of his army by imposing a rule of silence on them? Or does this sound more like a clever trick of the enemy?

Chapter~

9. Let your women keep silent

"… as also saith the law."

1 Corinthians 14:33b-35

I was a Sunday School kid, dropped off at the door, some-times by my faithful grandmother, and sometimes by the Sunday School bus. When I asked Jesus into my heart at daily Vacation Bible School, it had nothing at all to do with my parent's religious choices. This one was all mine. Later, I happily learned Bible verses to earn my way to summer Bible camp. Year after year, my hungry heart absorbed the stories of God's love and involvement with us here on earth. I loved the chapel sessions best when missionaries told of their adventures and the miracles God performed on their behalf.

At camp I made the commitment to serve God with my life, and for a season, I thought my service would surely be in mis-sions. I wanted to be where God was, and it surely looked to me like he was on the mission fields in other parts of the world. If at the time I also thought the mission field would give me more free-dom to minister as a female, I don't remember it being a conscious thought.

It was, however, this "calling" that caused me to enroll in the Baptist Bible College after high school. Here I was, ready to be-come a scholar of my particular brand of Christianity. Though I held my calling secret, I did resist all attempts to guide me into the Secretarial or Christian Education tracts.

As I confessed earlier, however, my more traditional choices of marriage and my firstborn interrupted my plans. I'm sure it also delayed my most serious encounters with gender inequity in the church.

I'm convinced there comes a time in all of our adult lives when we are faced with questions for which our childhood faith and our chosen denomination will not supply satisfying answers. We are confronted with truths that contradict the truths we thought we believed with all our hearts.

This is how I remember my first encounter with 1 Corinthians 14:33b-35 (NIV).

> *As in all the congregations of the saints, women should remain silent in the churches. They are not allowed to speak, but must be in submission, as the Law says. If they want to inquire about something, they should ask their own husbands at home; for it is disgraceful for a woman to speak in the church.*

"That can't be right, can it? What does it say?" I read it again, head spinning. "What about me? What about the times I've spoken in church?"

Was it a sin for me to stand up and report to sponsoring churches about the summer Bible Clubs I'd taught in their neighborhoods? Why didn't somebody warn me? And if it was a sin, why had it felt so right? Why had I received such positive affirmation from others in the congregation?

I remember wondering, "What on earth have I gotten myself into?" and even, "Why would a woman choose to be a part of a religion like this?"

Of course, I didn't mean me. I was already in. I may have felt trapped by the choices I had already made, but I was a Christian, no question about it. Did being a Christian mean I was obligated to follow this apparent legal restriction against speaking and even asking questions in church? Why do women go to Bible College? Is that a sin too?

What about the women missionaries who came to our church to bear witness of the things God is doing through their work in Africa and Bangladesh? What about the women who share their talent for singing special music, and often testify of God's love? And then there's the whole issue of Sunday School, where almost every teacher I know of is female. What about that?

I wish I could report my resolution came quickly. It didn't. How, after all was I to find the answer to this one if I can't even ask questions, except of my husband at home?

... "Why would a woman choose to be a part of a religion like this?"

Let me tell you, when I did start asking question of my then traditional-thinking husband, I encountered a lot more anger than I did answers.

It turns out the only really safe place, at least for a woman who lives and moves in traditional Christian circles, to question those traditions is in the secret places of the heart. She must become like Mary, the mother of Jesus, who pondered a secret knowing in her heart. Even though the things she knew were life-changing and world shattering, the very knowing that saves a soul from hell, for Mary it was better she did not speak her ponderings out loud.

So, like Mary, I went about the daily business of my life, raising children, serving in safe ways in the church and in the Christian school where my children were enrolled. I watched and listened for the truth about women in Christ's kingdom and his church. And finally, in desperation, I asked God to show me his heart toward women.

Just as the order of chapters in this book suggests, God did not begin his instruction to me by first showing me alternative readings for difficult passages in the New Testament. First I needed to learn and know by experience some basic principles of the gospel and the kingdom of God.

I began with my new understanding of creation, which allowed me to see myself as created in God's image, fully and equally called to participate in fruitfulness, dominion and subduing the earth. I learned that sin and the fall, not God's intent, were responsible for the deterioration of male/female relationships and roles. I became aware of women God called and used mightily in the stories of both the Old and New Testament.

I came to know God as a God of oneness and unity, as well as a God of grace. In other words, I came to understand these as major themes of the gospel. God desires us to be one, as Jesus and the Father are one, and, under the New Covenant, we live under grace and not under law. I am so grateful for this understanding, because by establishing these basic principles first, I was less likely to be misled when I tried to interpret some of the more difficult New Testament passages concerning women.

In other words, when I encountered these verses, I could hold them up to the scrutiny of the basic truth of the gospel. When a verse claims women must be silent and in subjection "as saith the law," I can ask questions based on what I know: "Am I under the law or under grace?"

And the whole weight of the New Testament gospel comes down on the side of grace.

Grace vs. Law

For the law was given by Moses, but grace and truth came by Jesus Christ (John 1:17).

The New Covenant is a Covenant of Grace, replacing the Old Covenant of Law.

"But before faith came, we were kept under guard by the law, kept for the faith which would afterward be revealed. Therefore the law was our tutor to bring us to Christ, that we might be justified by faith" (Gal. 3:23-24 NKJ).

Paul makes some extremely bold statements regarding the law and our new freedom in Christ. Setting himself as our example, he says,

"All things are lawful unto me, but all things are not expedient: all things are lawful for me, but I will not be brought under the power of any" (1Cor. 6:12, and) *"the letter (of the law) kills, but the Spirit gives life"* (2 Cor. 3:6).

Since these verses contain no restrictions as to gender, we can fairly assume they are also true for women. In fact, wouldn't it be liberating for Christian women, especially those who have been virtually killed, at least in spirit, by the letter of the law, to stand and read First Corinthians 6:12 out loud?

*All things are lawful unto me,
but all things are not expedient:
all things are lawful for me,
but I will not be brought under the power of any."*

One in Christ Jesus

The principle of unity, of being one with God and with one another, is a central theme of the gospel and of the New Testament. We can see in many New Testament passages God's desire that we be **one**. It is part of the prayer Jesus prayed for us in John 17, just before he went to the cross, " . . . that they may be one as we are ..." (verse 11 and 21-16).

To his disciples, who happened to be a small contingency of Jewish males, Jesus warned that others were coming into the kingdom. He used the metaphor of sheep from another sheep pen, but the meaning becomes clear in the light of the good news of grace that extends to people from every race and every social and economic class, both male and female. *"I have other sheep,"* he told the Jewish men, *"that are not of this sheep pen. I must bring them also. They too will listen to my voice, and there shall be* **one** *flock and* **one** *shepherd* (John 10:16).

Jesus invites "whosoever will" to come together as one body, one kingdom. His kingdom is unique in many ways, but one characteristic in particular is the inclusion of formerly excluded groups of people.

> *There is neither Jew nor Greek, there is neither bond nor free, there is neither male nor female: for ye are all* **one** *in Christ Jesus (Gal. 3:28).*

I have heard some objections to using Galatians 3:28 to argue for the equality of men and women. Many objectors claim that the verse is simply talking about salvation. In the earliest days of the gospel there was some debate about whether non-Jews could be saved. If the verse stopped there, if it only said, *"There is neither Jew nor Greek,"* perhaps the argument could be made that the verse is just talking about salvation. But the writer does not stop there. If the verse deals with salvation alone, then we must assume that there was some question about whether women and slaves were eligible to be saved. I don't think there was. Besides, an argument about who could and could not be saved would not fit within the context of this important letter to the Galatians.

Galatians is Paul's stern reminder that grace through faith, and not the law, is what grants entry into the kingdom of God. It is grace that invites Jews and Greeks, slaves and free people, men and women to full participation in the kingdom of God. In context, we are all one in Christ Jesus because grace turns us all into adult sons of God, joint heirs according to the promise (3:29). In Christ, we are no longer servants, no longer children, no longer excluded from the full rights of sons. All of us who were once excluded because we were not sons, now, because of grace, are fully included. We are all one in Christ Jesus (4:1-7).

But what about passages like 1 Corinthians 14:33b-35?

I still needed, as we all need, a plausible explanation of these verses that seem to contradict, not only the basic principles of the gospel, but also the surrounding verses and the understood intent of the author. I must remind the reader here, I make no attempt to offer exhaustive theological treatment of these passages. Nor do I offer original scholarship. Instead, I rely on the work of respected scholars and theologians, and I offer a pretty good list of additional sources in the appendix for those who wish to do further research.

My goal here is to demonstrate the possibility of legitimate alternate interpretations for the New Testament passages most often used to justify traditional ideas about the subordination of women.

Inconsistency with Paul's message

Most scholars agree the biggest problem with this passage is its inconsistency. For one thing, Paul has apparently assumed throughout his letter to the Corinthians that women were praying and prophesying in the church. In Chapter 11 he tells them they should cover their heads when they do it. In 14:26 he says " . . .*When you come together, everyone has a hymn, or a word of instruction, a revelation, a tongue or an interpretation. . .*" implying the women were actively contributing to the ministry in their meetings. For him to now to say women should keep silent and not speak in the churches is most inconsistent.

As we have already seen, one of Paul's primary messages to the church is that we are not under the law. (*"I do not frustrate the grace of God: for if righteousness come by the law, then Christ is dead in vain"* Gal. 2:21). Yet in verse 34 it seems he commands the obedience (submission) and silence of women *"as also saith the law."* Not only is this grossly inconsistent with Paul's other teaching, it begs the question, "What law?" There is no Old Testament law that commands the silence and submission of women.

In my research, I came across two possibilities for how these verses can be understood. Interestingly, and somewhat disturbingly, both explanations ultimately remove these verses from either Paul's advocacy or authorship. I found one explanation in the writings of Gilbert Bilezikian, the other in the writings of Gordon Fee.

Possibility One

In Gilbert Bilezikian's book, *Community 101, Reclaiming the Local Church as a Community of Oneness*, the author uses Paul's writings to demonstrate the apostle's strong support for unity and equality in worship. In Romans Paul deals with racial prejudice between Jews and Gentiles by saying, *"God shows no partiality"* (2:11 RSV). He also teaches that we are all one body with many members (12:4-5). As believers and members of the body, we have been given a variety of spiritual gifts, and are exhorted use them (12:6-8).

Bilezikian points out that logically, if Paul had intended any type of restriction to these statements about equal access and responsibility of gifts and ministry, here, "in a constitutional document of the church as influential as Paul's letter to the Romans" would have been the place to make it clear. No such restriction occurs in all of Romans. Rather, Paul's clear message is "for the universal participation in ministry" (85).

He continues his argument with a look at 1 Corinthians 12, where "Paul insists that God activates spiritual gifts in everyone" (85). Indeed, if you read chapter 12, you will find it hard to believe the same hand wrote the questionable verses in chapter 14. Chapter 12 basically says that God, by one and the same Spirit, freely gives gifts to every member of the body, and only as each believer uses his or her gifts freely can the body function as one. Bilezikian summarizes it this way: "Paul's emphatic message is that there are no exemptions or limitations to full participation in the life and ministries of the body" (86).

As to how this equal access to ministry might look, 1 Corinthians chapter 11 gives instructions to both men and women as they pray and prophesy. "The ministry functions were identical for the man and the woman, except for one difference, which had to do with attire" (86). This of course refers to the head coverings we talked about in the last chapter.

So we read along, sure that Paul is presenting a solid case for every believer receiving and using his or her spiritual gifts to strengthen the body of Christ. We read chapter 13, Paul's wonderful treatise on love. Then we read some specific instruction for seeking and using spiritual gifts in corporate worship, and we come to an abrupt halt at 14:33b-35.

> *As in all the churches of the saints, the women should keep*
> *silence in the churches. For they are not permitted to speak,*
> *but should be subordinate, as even the law says. If there is*
> *anything they desire to know, let them ask their husbands at*
> *home. For it is shameful for a woman to speak in church.*

In the King James version, the first word of the very next verse (36) is:

"What?"

That pretty well sums up my own response.

"What did he say? How could he be saying this after every thing else he just said?"

In sharp contrast to everything Paul has been saying, he now appears to be commanding the total silence of at least half of the members of the body. According to both Fee and Bilezikian, the language of prohibition against women speaking or even learning in the church seems to be complete and unrestricted.

Some have tried to limit the scope of the words by imagining a scenario where the women, seated off to the side or perhaps on the other side of a curtain, were talking loudly among themselves or shouting out inappropriate questions, and by their misbehavior were disturbing the order of the service. Paul is therefore, they say, only commanding the women straighten up and quit creating a disturbance.

According to Bilezikian, it goes deeper than that. The language used for this prohibition against women speaking or even learning in church (*not permitted ...to speak; ... commanded to be under obedience... a shame for women to speak in the church*) is meant to disqualify women from ministry. The stated justification for such restriction (*As in all the churches of the saints, ... as also saith the law*) is meant to imply total universal compliance (87). Of course, this prohibition, restricted or not, contradicts Paul's entire message thus far.

Bilezikian says the best explanation of the contradiction has more to do with punctuation than doctrine. Certain teachers (called Judaizers) were attempting to undermine Paul's work. Several times in his letter to the Corinthians, Paul quotes what the false teachers are saying and proceeds to point out the absurdity of their arguments.

Unlike our language, though, Paul did not have a device like quotation marks to designate when he was speaking with his own voice and when he was quoting others. He relied rather on the context of his words. Since everything leading up to 33b and 34 promotes a contrasting idea (verse 31 says all may prophesy, verses 32-33a says order is needed during worship) According to Bilezikian, Paul now has "the opportunity to tackle the contention caused in Corinth by false teachers . . .trying to impede women's ministries. So, he quoted their teaching to show how outrageous it was…" (88-89).

To summarize, these verses so absurdly contrast with the central idea of Paul's teaching as to suggest convincingly they were part of the author's argument for full and equal access and responsibility to minister according to one's spiritual gifts. In order to refute the false teaching that women were to be restricted from ministry and always silent and subject to men, Paul built a solid case for every member of the body using their gifts decently and in order. Then he stated the position of the false teachers to illustrate how far from the truth they had fallen.

Paul's response to the false ideas in verses 33b-35 is much like mine, and that of many readers of 1 Corinthians through the ages: "What? came the word of God out from you? or came it unto you only?" (verse 36).

Possibility Two

Many scholars theorize these two verses are not authentic, meaning they were not written by Paul. This is not a case of certain scholars disagreeing with what the verses say and trying to get rid of them. Instead, textual and contextual evidence strongly suggests the verses were not part of Paul's original epistle.

Mary Hayter, in *The New Eve in Christ*, says on page 128 that while we may doubt the passage is Pauline (written by Paul) still it cannot be dismissed because the church recognizes the document as authoritative. Her statement is consistent with the Catholic viewpoint, that both Scripture and church history form the basis for doctrine.

In his commentary on 1 Corinthians, Gordon Fee goes so far as to say, "there is substantial evidence that vv. 34-35 are not authentic" (697).

Besides its contextual inconsistencies (discussed above), Fee suggests other details of linguistics, syntax and style also indicate the passage was not part of Paul's original letter. For one, these verses do not deal with any kind of gifts or manifestations of the Spirit, even though that is Paul's topic. Also, most of the word usage in these verses is foreign to Paul's style (701-703).

But the most convincing argument, according to Fee, has to do with a historical inconsistency between various early manuscripts of the text. Apparently, the passage in question appears in one of two different locations in various manuscripts. While the passage is found in all existing manuscripts, in some it appears between verses 33 and 36, and in others it appears after verse 40.

Scholars are left to look for the reason for the displacement, which does not occur elsewhere in the New Testament (Fee, 700). If Paul wrote the text, no adequate reason has been found to say why a copyist would have moved the text from its original place. In fact, there is no historical precedent for that happening. Furthermore, in either place, these verses do more to interrupt Paul's argument than they do to help it. If the verses are removed, the argument flows smoothly from verse 33 to verse 36, and it makes more sense.

While there is no historical precedent for the displacement of original text, there is well documented evidence of other cases of marginal glosses making their way into the New Testament text. A marginal gloss is essentially a note written in the margin by a scholar, church official or translator. Sometimes copyists mistakenly incorporated these marginal notes into the text. Fee cites ...

"good historical reasons both for the gloss itself and for its dual position" (699). Scholars assume "the words were first written as a gloss in the margin by someone who, probably in light of 1 Timothy 2:9-15, felt the need to qualify Paul's instructions even further" (705).

Commentators who accept these verses as authentic are forced to do mental gymnastics in order to minimize the contradictions with Paul's message in the rest of the letter. Some theorize about different kinds of speech and different kinds of meetings, but the original language does not allow much room to maneuver. If it is authentic, it authoritatively says women must not speak at all in church services.

"Despite protests to the contrary, the "rule" itself is expressed absolutely. That is, it is given without any form of qualification . . . (meaning) all forms of speaking out in public" (706). (Furthermore, the author of the gloss) "seems intent on keeping women from joining in the vocal worship of the churches. The rule he wishes to apply, he sees as universal and supported by the law." (Fee, 708).

Of course, the reasons Paul supposedly gives for this absolute constraint against women speaking in public, *"as in all churches of the saints,"* and *"as also saith the law,"* are not arguments Paul would have used. Neither is there any law prohibiting women from speaking, at least not in the Old Testament.

We cannot, of course, be absolutely certain Paul did not write this passage. But the questions raised by this possible argument, and by the one before it, should be enough to make us very cautious, lest we enforce an "eternal prohibition" on women where none was intended.

By way of observation, few Christian denominations, even the most conservative among us, apply these verses literally or consistently in life and practice.

Chapter~

10. I Suffer Not a Woman

1Timothy 2:11-15

*Let the woman learn in silence with all subjection. But I
suffer not a woman to teach, nor to usurp authority over the
man, but to be in silence. For Adam was first formed, then
Eve. And Adam was not deceived, but the woman being
deceived was in the transgression. Notwithstanding she
shall be saved in childbearing, if they continue in faith and
charity and holiness with sobriety (1 Timothy 2:11-15)*

Paul and Jesus: Let the woman learn!

My first breakthrough when confronted with 1 Timothy 2 came
when I learned more about Paul's choice of words as he addressed
the issue of women learning and teaching and exercising authority. Later I leaned more about the historical context of Paul's unusual
advice to Timothy and the church at Ephesus.

With all my traditional expectations intact, I used to read these
verses as one more bullet in the arsenal of those who would silence women. It seems to hold all women eternally responsible for
the sin of Eve in the garden, never mind the grace provided in
Jesus Christ. With a kind of selective amnesia about Adam's sin, it
seemed the Apostle here advocates for women the eternal punishment of silence and submission as penalty for Eve's sin. In addition,

it sounds like he proposes a different means of salvation for women, childbearing!

"Well, it's no wonder!" I remember yelling under my breath to no one in particular. "But if the blood of Christ is not sufficient to cover the sin of Eve, how can we expect to be redeemed by childbirth? And if we are to be eternally punished, why stop at silence and submission?"

Even in my calmer moods, one thing I could never figure out was why the Apostle Paul seemed to be so at odds with Jesus in his attitude toward women. My traditional reading of 1 Timothy 2:11-15, the only reading I knew, painted Paul's ideas in such sharp contrast to the life and practices of Jesus, I was tempted –now and then—to dismiss Paul as a hopeless woman hater. This, however, created a huge disturbance to my firmly-held belief in the truth and inerrancy of Scriptures. Later, however, I came to see the traditional reading of this passage as impossibly inconsistent with the apostle's own central purpose and teachings.

With the help of some contemporary scholars and theologians, thankfully, I've been able to take another look at the language and context of these verses, and at least in my own mind, let the Apostle off the hook. I no longer believe Paul inserted his own disdain for women into his rules for the early church. I no longer secretly suspect him of interrupting what God intended for the role of women in the church.

Earlier we looked at Jesus' support of Mary when she desired the better part, to sit at his feet and learn (Luke 10:38-42). We said her position at Jesus' feet was the same as that of a young rabbinic student. Paul himself once studied at the feet of Gamaliel (Acts 22:3). If we look again at the language of First Timothy, we see Paul following Christ's example when he said, *"Let the women learn."*

Demeanor of a Good Student

The second part of Paul's command to let the women learn concerns the demeanor a woman should adopt when learning.

Mary, seated at the feet of Jesus, sets a precedent Paul follows in his letter to Timothy. Sitting in silence to learn, the norm for male students of Scriptures, had not been for females. Jesus, however, said it was better for Mary to sit in silence at his feet and learn, than to be busy with much household serving (Spencer, 57-63). Paul told Timothy to *"Let a woman learn in silence with all submission"* (1Tim. 2:11).

Rather than making a rule about women keeping silent in the church, I believe Paul was agreeing with Jesus, that women need the opportunity to sit quietly at the feet of Jesus, to learn in peace, to leave off traditional expectations about "women's work" and become students of the kingdom of God.

Learning in order to teach

Aida Spencer points out it was also presumed a learner would eventually become a teacher. The rabbis taught that a good learner learns in order to teach (Spencer, p.85). Paul too assumes this:

"And the things you have heard me say in the presence of many witnesses entrust to reliable men who will also be qualified to teach others" (2 Tim. 2:2 NIV).

Note that the correct translation should be "Entrust to reliable people," not just males! See "Men Spells Women Too" at the end of this chapter. See also Hebrews 5:12-14.

Gordon Fee's *New International Biblical Commentary, 1 and 2 Timothy, Titus* says the manner in which she learns is the focus of this sentence. "But she is to **learn**, not 'in silence' (that is, without speaking), as some would have it, but 'in a quiet demeanor' (72). The word for "in silence" is *"hesuchia,"* a word that also appears in 1 Timothy 2:2, *"that we may lead a quiet and peaceable life in all godliness and honesty."*

The many interesting connotations of this Greek word instruct us about the way women should learn. In Acts 21, Paul is in the protective custody of soldiers because of an angry mob outside the temple in Jerusalem. Paul asks permission of the commander to speak and address the crowd. After quieting the crowd somewhat, Paul begins to address them. But 22:2 says, *And when they heard that he spake in the Hebrew tongue to them, they kept the more silence (hesuchia)"* Here the word denotes the quiet respect of an audience deciding not to disagree but to listen.

In 2 Thessalonians, Paul rebukes those who *"walk disorderly, working not at all, but are busybodies"* (3:11). He then exhorts them, instead of this bad behavior, they should *"with quietness (hesuchia) . . . work, and eat their own bread"* (12). This verse, like 1 Timothy 2:2, is addressed to both males and females. Quietness, peacefulness, harmony and agreement are qualities God seeks in all of his people.

Paul repeats the word *hesuchia* in verse 12 of First Timothy 2, when he says he is not allowing women to teach or usurp authority *"but to be in silence."* In other words, verse 11 says, "**do** allow women to learn, but like every believer, it is good for her to learn with a spirit of quietness, in harmony and agreement.

Peter confirms the idea, this is a proper demeanor for women when he says her:

> *"... beauty should not come from outward adornment, (but from her) ...inner self, the unfading beauty of a gentle and quiet (hesuchia) spirit, which is of great worth in God's sight"* (1 Peter 3:3-4, NIV).

Peter is addressing women, but as we have observed, a gentle and quiet spirit is of great worth in God's sight, whether in a man or a woman.

Compare Isaiah 66:1-2:

> *"This is what the LORD says: 'Heaven is my throne, and the earth is my footstool. Where is the house you will build for me? Where will my resting place be? Has not my hand made all these things, and so they came into being?' declares the LORD. 'This is the one I esteem: he who is humble and contrite in spirit, and trembles at my word.'"* (NIV)

God holds in high esteem all those who are quiet and humble in spirit. It is not a gender specific quality. Quietness and peacefulness are qualities all believers might seek, if our desire is to please God. How much more should those who have much to learn, who wish to prepare themselves for effective ministry, be full of humility and quiet submission.

Be silent, or be at peace?

It should also be pointed out, when Paul wanted to silence certain people because of the heresy they were teaching, he used different words all together.

> *For there are many unruly and vain talkers and deceivers, specially they of the circumcision: Whose mouths must be stopped who subvert whole houses, teaching things which they ought not, for filthy lucre's sake....* (Titus 1:11-14).

The Greek word here is *epistomizo*, to bridle, to stop the mouth, to reduce to silence. Paul does not hesitate to use strong language for these unruly talkers and deceivers. He does not however, use this word or this command when instructing Timothy concerning the female believers in his congregation.

He uses the word *hesuchia, which is* most likely related to the verb *hesuchazo,* meaning *"I am silent. I rest. I cease from labor"* (Spencer, 75-76). The definition calls to mind Mary and Martha. Martha was very busy with her much serving. Jesus gave Mary permission to let go of her traditional responsibility and sit at his feet, to rest from her labor, to learn from him.

In all submission

Being in quietness as she learns includes the idea of being in submission. The writer does not say to whom she should submit. According to Gordon Fee's commentary on the text, the idea that Paul is here commanding wives to be submissive to their husbands is unsubstantiated by the text (Fee, 72). Paul is talking about the manner in which women should learn, presumably from their male teachers. He requires nothing more of female learners than would automatically be required of male learners. Anyone who wants to learn should be willing to sit at the feet of the teacher in all quietness and submission, just as Mary sat at the feet of Jesus.

The opposite of this kind of quietness and submissiveness might be such things as envy and selfish ambition, the things James warns about when he compares Godly wisdom to that which is earthly. He exhorts Christians to be filled with Godly wisdom:

> For where you have envy and selfish ambition, there you
> find disorder and every evil practice. But the wisdom that
> comes from heaven is first of all pure; then peace-loving,
> considerate, submissive, full of mercy and good fruit,
> impartial and sincere (James 3:16-17 NIV).

But I suffer not a woman to teach

In contrast to the language of verse 11 (*"Let the women learn,"*) *the phrase, "But I suffer not a woman to teach,"* is less of a command and more of an explanation. *"But I suffer not"* is best translated "I am not permitting" which suggests something Paul intends for the current situation in Ephesus (Fee, 72). The idea here is the situation demanded a temporary withdrawal of the license to teach among Ephesian women. We will look further into the specific situation in the church at Ephesus in the coming paragraphs.

Overpowering Destructive Authority

The next phrase, *"nor to usurp authority over the man,"* most commentators agree, carries with it the idea of domineering (Fee, 73). The word translated "to usurp authority" is the Greek word *"authenteo"* or *"authentein"* which does not appear in any other New Testament text. If Paul meant to say a woman could never have authority or power (*exousia,* a word Paul uses on several other occasions) over a man, he would not likely have chosen this obscure word to make his meaning clear.

When no biblical passages help us determine the meaning of a word, scholars and translators look to the literature of the period to try to determine the best translation or meaning. In the centuries before Christ, the word *"authentein"* meant, *"to be the originator of a murder."* Later, during the first century, it was used in a context meaning, *"to be the author of."* After the second or third century the word had come to mean "to usurp authority" or to "domineer."

Richard and Catherine Clark Kroeger's book, *I Suffer Not A Woman; Rethinking 1 Timothy 2:11-15 in Light of Ancient Evidence* (Baker, 1992) helped me better understand the specific heresies present in Ephesus at the time of Paul's writing. The Diana Cult apparently carried with it the idea of a female originator of all things. The heresy, according to the Kroegers, was making its way into the Christian church and claiming Eve was the originator of Adam, and thus of all humankind.

Her name, after all, means "The Mother of All Living." Since one of the contemporary meanings of the word *"authentein"* is *"to be the author of,"* they suggest that in order to come against this specific heresy, Paul said, *"I do not allow woman to teach that she is the author or originator of man."* The biggest advantage I see to this interpretation is that it fits nicely into the context when the next verse is*: "For Adam was formed first, then Eve."*

If Paul wanted to dispel the notion that Eve's title as Mother of All Living gave her supremacy over Adam as his source of being, it is most appropriate for him to remind them that, according to Genesis, Adam was formed first, then Eve.

Aida Spencer looks at contemporary texts to determine the word "authentein" was used when rulers overpowered their subjects to the point of murdering or destroying them (86-87). Jesus talked about a similar negative concept of authority when the disciples had been worrying about who would be greatest among them:

*Jesus called them together
and said, "You know that
the rulers of the Gentiles
lord it over them, and their
high officials exercise
authority over them. Not so
with you. Instead, whoever
wants to become great among you must be your servant, and
whoever wants to be first must be your slave - just as the
Son of Man did not come to be served, but to serve, and to
give his life as a ransom for many.' (Matt. 20:25-28 NIV).*

*... Christ-like authority takes on
the qualities of humility and
love, and serves its subjects.*

Jesus understood what was in the heart of man. He offered a
view of leadership and authority in sharp contrast to the ways of
the world. Worldly authority "lords over," demeans and destroys
its subjects. Christ-like authority takes on the qualities of humility
and love, and serves its subjects.

In the same spirit, Peter instructs those who would be shepherds or overseers:

*Be shepherds of God's flock that is under your care, serving
as overseers - not because you must, but because you are
willing, as God wants you to be; not greedy for money, but
eager to serve; not lording it over those entrusted to you, but
being examples to the flock (1 Peter 5:2-3 NIV).*

"Leadership which overpowers and destroys is never ap-
proved by Christ for either men or women" (Spencer, 87). For me,
in the light of this new understanding of the cultural situation (false
teachings among the believers at Ephesus) and of the meaning of
the word used here for authority, I can see an alternate meaning
for the passage. Paul is **not** commanding all women not to teach or
preach, and he is **not** telling us a woman may never have authority over a man. Rather, he is telling us, women in Ephesus must
learn the truth in quiet submission before they presume to teach,
and they should be careful not to use their authority "in a destruc-
tive way" (Spencer, 88).

Of course, as we observed, next Paul brings the creation story
into the narrative: *"For Adam was formed first, then Eve."* Some traditionalists have theorized that he mentions Adam was formed
first to say Adam was superior, and to give a reason for Eve's en-

forced subjection to him. Paul, however, does not elaborate.

Observe, when the author brings up the order of creation in 1 Corinthians 11:8-9 (woman is "of the man" and was created "for the man") he makes no reference to submission. And don't forget, he adds verses 11-12 as if to guard against such a misapplication: *"... For as the woman is of the man, even so is the man also by the woman; but all things of God."* (Fee, 74).

The point Paul seems to be going for is in the next verse, (14): *"And Adam was not deceived, but the woman being deceived was in the transgression."*

Eve, after all, *was* deceived and became a sinner. He is not saying Adam did not sin, nor is he saying Eve's sin was greater. He is simply reminding us by way of warning, a woman has as much potential to be deceived and fall into sin as any of the men.

I'm just a sinner, saved by . . . childbearing?

The next verse has sent readers and scholars scrambling for an explanation for centuries. *"Notwithstanding she shall be saved in childbearing,"* has produced many theories about what the apostle might really have meant.

According to Gordon Fee, two of the most prominent theories are, at best, a stretch. The first theory is women will henceforth be saved from the curse of pain in childbearing. Two problems arise from this theory. For one, many Christian women have suffered and died in childbirth. For another, Paul always uses the word here translated "saved" to refer to redemption. He uses a different word altogether when he means saved from danger or peril.

The second theory is women will be saved by *the childbirth*. Because Jesus was born, women can now be saved. One problem with this theory is vague language, and it takes a serious stretch to make it say this. Another problem is the contradiction with a basic principle of redemption. The New Testament is consistent in its message that redemption came through Christ's atoning death on the cross, and not through Mary's participation in the incarnation.

If Paul wanted to point to a woman's redemption, he could have done so in more clear ways. More likely, her redemption is simply assumed in this passage, since Paul is talking to and about believing women. There is no other instance when Paul refers to redemption by referring to Mary's act of childbirth. Indeed, Paul would not say that redemption in any way comes through Mary. And the language cannot in any way be understood to mean "Mary's Child" (Fee, 75).

Paul is concerned because these women are being deceived and then participating in the spreading of heresy. He reminds us, although Adam was created first, Eve was the first to be deceived. This serves as a warning: women, like men, can be deceived and fall into sin. The consequences of such sin are very great, as Eve's sin demonstrates. But, coming back to the women at Ephesus, he says though they are in transgression, they will be saved.

Then, of course, he surprises us by adding the words "in childbearing." So much has been written about the possible meanings of this word, it seems almost foolish for us to try to make sense of it. Gordon Fee offers at least a reasonable explanation.

Fee feels that Paul meant women could be saved from the danger of deception and transgression (like Eve's) if they would give themselves to good deeds. Because of Paul's later instruction concerning younger widows, it appears Paul considers being married and bearing children to be good deeds for women, and also he sees these as a protection against potential transgressions.

Besides, they get into the habit of being idle and going about from house to house. And not only do they become idlers, but also gossips and busybodies, saying things they ought not to. So I counsel younger widows to marry, to have children, to manage their homes and to give the enemy no opportunity for slander (1 Timothy 5:13-14 NIV).

Doctrinally, Paul would not suggest anyone is saved or redeemed by their good deeds. To make that point, Paul adds the qualification, "… *if they continue in **faith** and charity and holiness with sobriety*" (1 Timothy 2:15). Paul is presuming the women in question were already women of faith.

The "I will" or I want of verses 8 and 9, where Paul desires men pray with lifted hands and women adorn themselves modestly, is the same as the "I want" of 5:14, where he says, "*I will therefore that the younger women marry …*"

Paul is not making a law. There is no hint of command in these phrases. He is giving the **wise counsel** of a trusted teacher and elder.

In Titus, he instructs the older women to teach the younger ones to love their husbands and to be keepers at home. To the Ephesians, he says they can be protected (saved) from falling into deception and sin if they will concentrate on such good deeds as loving their husbands, bearing children, being keepers at home, while continuing in their faith (for salvation) and also in love and holiness with propriety.

I ran across another reasonable explanation in *The Study Bible for Women* edited by Catherine Clark Kroeger, Mary Evans and Elaine Storkey. In the footnote to 1 Timothy 2:15, the editors say the phrase alludes to Genesis 3:15-16 where Eve is promised greater pain in childbirth. The prevalent teachings of the Gnostics made false claims that condemned childbearing, and some even claimed that a woman could not gain eternal life.

> *"This section refutes the Gnostic teaching by affirming that any woman may be saved as she is, distinct from men, and retaining the capacity to bear children, only on the condition that she lives as befits Christian people"* (page 442).

"Men" spells "Women" too?

As in many other passages, the word "men" in 2 Tim. 2:2 ("And the things you have heard me say in the presence of many witnesses entrust to reliable men (anthropos) who will also be qualified to teach others") cannot always be understood to mean males.

In translating Greek to English, some meaning has been lost. Translators have chosen to use the word **man** or **men,** whether or not the Greek specified man as in male, or man as in humankind. In most cases, the word "anthropos" meaning "man-faced, i.e. a human being" and therefore including both male and female, is translated man (346 times in the KJV New Testament) or men (197 times) instead of person or people.

In addition, of course, the word "aner" which actually does mean "a man, as an individual male" is also translated man or men. When we read in English, we can't tell if it means man (male) or man (human being).

Other words compound the problem. For example, the word "oudeis" means "not even one man, woman, or thing, nobody." Almost always, the word is translated "no man."

The word "tis," meaning "some or any person or object" is almost always translated "any man." The word "hekastos" which means "each and every" becomes, for some reason, "every man." It's no wonder we might have gotten a decidedly masculine picture of the people and events of the New Testament.

This is not because of the inspiration of the Scriptures, but because of the decisions of the translators. I wish I could recommend an easy solution. Until someone dares to undertake a new translation to more accurately reflect what the original writers meant to say with regard to male and female, readers will have to check outside sources and helps to get a true picture.

I use a Greek/English translation and the "Show Strong's Numbers" feature on Verse Search (computer software by Bible Research Systems, Austin, Texas. 1996) when I need clarification.

Note: Since the original writing of this section, Zondervan Publishing has released *Today's New International Version* (TNIV), starting with an updated translation of the New Testament, and now including the whole Bible, which improves the accuracy of translation from the *New International Version* (NIV). In the words of The Committee on Bible Translation taken from the introduction to the TNIV, "The first concern of the translators has been the accuracy of the translation and its faithfulness to the meaning of the biblical writers." Thankfully, that accuracy has included differentiating between references to human beings, male and female, and references to males exclusively. I rejoice in the faithfulness of men and women who have labored to put such a valuable translation into our hands, and I pray it will bless many of you as it has blessed me.

PART 3

Eve Redeemed

Chapter~

11. Second Adam and Second Eve

Reading Madeleine L' Engle's *The Rock That Is Higher, Story as Truth*, I began to meditate on restoration and redemption. I began to see how Jesus had come to break down walls. He broke down the walls that separated humanity from God. The veil in the temple was torn in two the moment Jesus gave up his life for us. He broke down the walls that separated Jews from Gentiles, slaves from free people, and males from females (Galatians 3:28).

Obvious as it seems to me today, I only then began to recognize that restoration and redemption are main themes of Scripture, and are in fact, the main purpose of Christ's incarnation. Jesus came to restore what the worm has eaten, (Joel 2:25) to redeem us from the curse of the law.

I remember learning, in a class on human development, about an experiment involving fish in an aquarium. The fish were accustomed to receiving food from above, when scientists sprinkled it into the tank. Then one day a glass partition was placed in the tank. From then on, during phase one of the experiment, the food was sprinkled only on one side of the glass. The fish on the other side, seeing it through the glass, attempted to swim to it and feed themselves. Each time they bumped their noses against the glass. Each time they went hungry. Eventually, they quit trying to reach the food.

For phase two of the experiment, the glass partition was removed. Food continued to come from above, but now nothing separated the food from the fish. No matter. The fish did not eat. In the presence of plenty of food the fish died of starvation, not because of reality, but because of what they believed, based on past experience.

I know Christian women who have created fairly satisfying lives on one side of the glass that separates them from equal access to the gifts and ministry of the church. For many, even if they learn the glass partition has been removed, even if they realize Jesus himself is the one who removed it, their lives won't change much. For they have become content in a world of their own making. Their responses have been conditioned by the presence of the dividing wall between male and female.

"But wait!" I want to cry out. "We are not fish!" If the earth is mine, and all the fullness thereof, why should I be content to dwell within a glass box with man-made walls? If Jesus says, "Woman, thou art loosed," why should I allow myself to be constrained by the traditions of men?

Thankfully, with the help of Scripture and the Holy Spirit, I am coming to see that as a female I am not exempt from the restoration and redemption Jesus provides. Even the Old Testament prophets speak of the restoration of women to the fullness of God's purposes. Zechariah talks about God's return to Zion to dwell in Jerusalem,

> *... the City of Truth, and the Mountain of the Lord Almighty... This is what the LORD Almighty says: "Once again men and women of ripe old age will sit in the streets of Jerusalem, each with cane in hand because of his age. The city streets will be filled with boys and girls playing there (Zechariah 8:3-5).*

This speaks to me of the promise of equality and partnership restored between men and women. As one who has been excluded from full participation in my faith, I too can look to the work of Jesus my redeemer and be set free.

Traditional beliefs about men and women have sometimes gone so far as to say a woman does not even have authority over her own self. As we have seen, that was indeed true under the Old Covenant. A father or a husband could nullify a vow made by the woman under his care, whether a daughter or a wife. Once, among God's people, a Father's inheritance always went to the first-born son.

But just as the prophets looked ahead to the time when the Messiah would come and free Israel from its oppression, some of the words of the prophets gave particular comfort to women. My favorite is Zechariah 9:9:

> *Rejoice greatly, O Daughter of Zion! Shout, Daughter of Jerusalem! See, your king comes to you, righteous and having salvation, gentle and riding on a donkey, on a colt, the foal of a donkey (NIV).*

Jesus took special care to see this prophecy fulfilled. As he entered Jerusalem just before his crucifixion, he sent his disciples with specific instructions to find a particular donkey with a colt.

> *"All this was done that it might be fulfilled which was spoken by the prophet, saying: 'Tell the daughter of Zion, 'Behold, your King is coming to you, lowly, and sitting on a donkey, a colt, the foal of a donkey'" (Matt. 21:1-5).*

Finally, I see it. I understand, as if for the first time, the redemption Jesus has offered me from the beginning. Jesus intentionally included me, and all women like me, in the restoration he provided. Though my teachers may have neglected to show me, God in his love and faithfulness reveals it to me in full measure, pressed down and shaken together. Having just read the passages in Zechariah and Matthew, here is my prayer as recorded in my journal on April 19, 1996:

> *My Jesus, I will never again doubt that you came to set the captives free, and that your purpose included me, the captive female. You came to break the power of sin, even the first sin of Adam and Eve. You came to ransom all of us from the curse.*
>
> *Forgive me for allowing my culture and tradition to speak louder to me than your Word speaks. Whether any man ever agrees, I will walk in the freedom you came to provide. Help me to also walk in your grace and in your love.*

For in this moment, this reading of the word, I knew. The sin of Eve, while devastating in its effect on mankind after Eden, does not trump the grace of God. The sacrificial love of Jesus extends intentionally to the daughters of Eve. He is righteous and gentle and he has salvation for us. He came to redeem us, as women, from every consequence of Eve's initial sin. He came to restore to us everything we had lost.

As I meditated on the restorative power of Jesus, I continued to write in my journal the words that became the seed for this chapter, and in many ways, this book:

> *… Now I want to introduce a new train of thought. Jesus is called the second Adam. The church must be the second Eve. In the first Adam, all die. But in Christ is life and liberty. What about Eve?*

If Jesus is the second Adam, who is the second Eve?

In addition to the bridegroom, Jesus is called the Second Adam. By implication, if Jesus is The Second Adam, we, the bride of Christ, could be called *The Second Eve*.

~The Second Eve~

Into death's deep sleep he's fallen
Second Adam looking for his bride.
Second spear drives deep and pierces.
Sacred love spills from his side.

Born of water, blood and spirit,
Shaped on ancient Rock of God
For himself he formed a helper
Fit for him, his church, his bride.

B.B. (2002)

Just as the first Eve emerged from the wounded side of the first Adam, so we, the second Eve, emerge redeemed from the wounded side of Jesus, the second Adam. Now the bridegroom invites us, his church, the redeemed bride, into intimate union with him. It is from this intimacy with Christ that new life comes, first to our own lives, and then to the lives of those who are touched by our testimony.

First Adam and Second Adam

*And so it is written, The first man Adam was made a living
soul; the last Adam was made a quickening spirit. ...The
first man is of the earth, earthy; the second man is the Lord
from heaven (1 Cor. 15:45-47).*

Romans 5:12-17 speaks of sin and death entering the world
through the first Adam, so that *"death reigned from Adam to Moses."*
Adam, it says, is *"the figure of him that was to come"* meaning Jesus.
Fortunately, it says, the gift of God is not like the offense of Adam,
which caused the death of many. *"How much more did God's grace
and the gift that came by the grace of the one man, Jesus Christ, overflow
to the many!"*

First Eve, Second Eve

Reading Romans 5 with my journal by my side, I found confirmation of my liberty in Jesus Christ, the second Adam. The first
Eve, made in God's image to share in the work God planned for
humankind, had fallen from grace. She became a **sinner**, incurred
the **wrath of God**, and was **separated from God**. In the centuries
that followed, she was made **powerless** by the power of sin. Now,
in Christ, the second Adam, her plight, and mine, has changed.

*You see, at just the right time, when we were still
powerless, Christ died for the ungodly.
... God demonstrates his own love for us in this: While we
were still **sinners,** Christ died for us. Since we have now
been justified by his blood, how much more shall we be saved
from **God's wrath** through him! For if, when we were
God's enemies, we were **reconciled to him** through the
death of his Son, how much more, having been reconciled,
shall we be **saved through his life!** Not only is this so, but
we also rejoice in God through our Lord Jesus Christ,
through whom we have now received reconciliation (Romans
5:6-11 NIV, emphasis mine).*

I am tempted to insert the word "women" after every "we"
as in, "While we women were still powerless" and "sinners." In
other words, I have no trouble reading this passage as the emanci-
pation of women in Christ. Christ died for us, and we women are
saved from God's wrath through him. Once his enemies, we women

have been reconciled to him. And no traditional doctrine about the place of women will ever again have the power to rob me from the understanding that as a woman of God, I am invited to full participation in the kingdom of God.

I wrote a declaration in my journal in response to these powerful things God was showing me. I want to declare it again for myself and for all women who have been redeemed by the blood of the lamb.

> *Our bridegroom, the one who has declared his everlasting love for us and betrothed us to him, has made us into a spotless bride. He has lifted the weight of centuries of sin from our shoulders. He has reconciled us to himself. He has redeemed us, now and forever. He has restored to us the power he intended for us in creation (5/14/96).*

Interestingly, it is in the New Testament instruction to husbands to love their wives as Christ loved the church that we find the language describing Christ as bridegroom and we, the church, as his bride.

> *Husbands, love your wives, even as Christ also loved the church, and gave himself for it (her); That he might sanctify and cleanse it (her) with the washing of water by the word, That he might present it (her) to himself a glorious church (or bride) . . . (Eph. 5:25-27, insertions mine).*

The first Eve was created to be the bride and help-meet of the first Adam. As the bride of the first Adam, Eve was to work with Adam, along side him, to subdue the earth, and also to *be fruitful and multiply, and replenish the earth* (Gen. 1:28). After the fall, of course, the image of the bride was tarnished by sin and deception. Redemption, however, reverses the damage done by the fall. Christ gave himself for her in order to sanctify and cleanse her and present her to himself as a glorious bride.

As the bride of Christ, Eve's image is redeemed. She is made clean and presented to the bridegroom without spot or wrinkle. Clearly the church, regardless of gender, is to become the bride of the second Adam, or Christ.

> *Wherefore, my brethren, ye also are become dead to the law by the body of Christ; that ye should be married to another,*

even to him who is raised from the dead, that we should bring forth fruit unto God (Rom. 7:4).

The relationship between the Second Adam and the Second Eve

New Testament passages often compare the relationship between men and women, especially in marriage, to the relationship between Christ and the church. It seems to me, if we misunderstand God's ideal of relationship between men and women, we will also misunderstand our roles and the ideal of relationship between Christ and the church.

Could we use our imaginations to carry the comparison out to its limits? How would the comparisons look if we approach them as traditionalists? For example, if we were to return to the idealized American 1950's model of husband-wife relationships, would Jesus be the husband who works outside the church/home, leaving the care of young believers almost exclusively to his stay-at-home bride?

Could we see the church as the daughter of the Old Covenant who has moved from the control of her father (God and the law) to the control of her husband, God's son? As the traditional bride, is the church (bride) responsible primarily to bear children (as sinners saved by childbearing?). Is she to stay home and raise the offspring and care for the house? Is the church asked to keep silent in submission to her husband, Jesus? Is the church asked to limit her sphere of influence to the home (in this case, the church) and her duties to traditional women's work?

In contrast, what if we make the same comparisons using the equality model for husbands and wives? Would we then see a model of the church invited into a relationship of equality with our savior and bridegroom? Could we, the church, embrace the marvelous grace of God and see ourselves as joint heirs with Jesus? Could we marvel with our brothers and sisters as Jesus humbles himself and washes our feet and calls us his friends? Could we respond in love to him when he invites us into the same oneness he shares with his father God?

I, for one, can believe him when he declares to us, male and female, *"Wherefore thou art no more a servant, but a son; and if a son, then an heir of God through Christ"* (Gal. 4:7). Shall we not carry on for him, our brother, our friend, our husband, the work he has begun? Shall we not receive the power of the Holy Spirit to be his witnesses in the earth?

> *"In the last days, God says, I will pour out my Spirit on all people. Your sons and daughters will prophesy ...Even on my servants, both men and women, I will pour out my Spirit in those days, and they will prophesy" (Acts 2:17-18, NIV)*

The feminine helps express who we are as the bride of Christ

The New Testament is certainly not devoid of the feminine in its references to God. It uses marriage, the intimate coming to-gether of male and female, to describe the mystery of our relationship to Christ. The relationship between a husband and a wife serves as a metaphor for the relationship between Christ and his people. Christ is the husband, and we, his people, are the bride.

If we disregard the feminine and misunderstand the femi-nine role as God ordained it, we will also fail to understand our role as the body and bride of Christ.

The marriage of the masculine with the feminine brings forth life

As the bride of the first Adam, Eve was told with Adam to *be fruitful and multiply, and replenish the earth, and subdue it.* After the fall the image of the bride was tarnished by sin and deception.

As the bride of Christ, however, her image is redeemed. She is made clean, and presented to the bridegroom without spot or wrinkle.

Some people may not be totally comfortable with carrying the metaphor of Christ as bridegroom and the church as bride be-yond the wedding day. But the imagery of bearing fruit is abundant in Scriptures (Rom. 7:4).

As the bride of Christ, the church (the second Eve) is to join with Christ by the power of the Holy Spirit, to *be fruitful* — to bring forth fruit worthy of the kingdom. As bride she is invited to become one with Christ, the Son of God. It is only in their oneness that the bride and groom can together bring forth life.

The surprisingly feminine image of the new birth

Jesus himself chose to use markedly feminine imagery to de-scribe our entry into the kingdom of God at the moment of our redemption. "I tell you the truth," he said, *"No one can see the kingdom of God unless he is born again"* (John 3:3, NIV).

He went on to explain to Nicodemus that being born again was not entering a second time into our mother's womb, not being born of flesh, but being born of the Spirit.

Birth, unquestionably a feminine process, describes the entry of a believer from the place of darkness to the place of light. The person who is born again enters the kingdom of God. He or she is born of the Spirit of God this time, born not of woman but of God. Do you begin to see why it takes both male and female to fully bear the image of God?

The one giving birth when we are born of the Spirit, is God

If we allow ourselves to fully embrace an understanding of the feminine imagery in being born of God, we are invited into an experience of entering fully into God, being surrounded by God and encompassed about by God.

Jesus chose birth imagery for a purpose. I doubt he would object to us using our imagination to draw parallels between our new birth into his kingdom and the miraculous experience of childbirth.

The Scriptures tell us God knew us when we were being formed in the womb. The spiritual parallel allows us to be known by God while we are being drawn into fellowship with him. We are incubated in a sacred place and prepared for entrance into new life as sons and daughters of God.

Now imagine, as you were being formed in the spirit, you were in the very womb of God. Imagine that God knows you intimately, and when the fullness of time is come, you enter again into the world through the narrow gate as a new creature, born of God, and born of the Spirit.

Indeed, there may be much we have missed in our understanding of God and of the Spirit because of our failure to include the feminine in our understanding. There seems to be more at stake in learning to reconcile male and female in the body of Christ than deciding whether or not a woman can hold an office or preach a sermon.

Chapter~

12. Eve Redeemed

Redemption changed our relationship to God and to each other

I do not remember the first time I heard about the ancient Jewish prayer in which a man thanks God each day for his good fortune that he was not born a Gentile, he was not born an ignorant man, and he was not born a woman. I have come to understand from Bible scholars like Aida B. Spencer that the intent of the prayer was not to denigrate women as much as it was to express gratitude for the right to study the law of God (Spencer, 64). Because I had seen the 1983 movie *Yentl*, the tragic tale of a Jewish girl who so desperately wanted to study the Torah that she chose to dress and live as a man, I was emotionally prepared to understand why a devout Jewish man might utter such a prayer.

I was not, however, emotionally prepared to read what some early church fathers thought and said about women. Reading Mary Hayter's book, *The New Eve in Christ*, I encountered these disturbing bits of history. Aquinas viewed woman as a "misbegotten male" (84). He saw her as "inferior to man at the level of her soul, as well as in the physical imperfection of her body." As such, he believed, "...woman was made *only* to assist in procreation" (page 101).

While Augustine did acknowledge that a husband and wife together express the image of God, he said that when assigned the role of helpmate, "...she is not the image of God; but as far as the man is concerned, he is by himself the image of God, just as fully and completely as when he and the woman are joined together into one" (page 101).

Earlier church leaders Chrysostom and Tertullian had their own negative take on the female side of humanity. Looking at Eve's sin in the garden, Chrysostom concluded "the whole female sex was shown to be 'weak and fickle, …the whole female race transgressed" (page 103). Holding forth the "negative image of Eve as beguiling temptress, according to Tertullian's interpretation of Genesis, the daughters of Eve should wear penitential garb to remind themselves that it was through Eve that sin entered the world." Indeed, "Tertullian blamed woman for the sufferings of mankind and of Christ himself."

Hayter includes this quote from Tertullian's writings:

You are the one who opened the door to the Devil, you are the one who first plucked the fruit of the forbidden tree, you are the one who first deserved the divine law: you are the one who persuaded him whom the Devil was not strong enough to attack. All too easily you destroyed the image of God, man. Because of your desert, that is, death, even the Son of God had to die (103).

It's hard to say where Tertullian's assumption originated. He says, "the Devil was not strong enough to attack" Adam, and was thus obliged to get Eve to do it for him. As we discussed in Chapter 3, the Devil did not think himself too weak to attack God's favored servant, Job. Neither did he feel too week to tempt Jesus himself in the wilderness. On these only other times the Bible gives an actual account of Satan's temptation, the tempter chooses to go straight to the top.

These harsh words reinforce to us that the consequences of sin in the garden changed our relationship to God and to each other. I believe the redemption that came through Jesus Christ was intended to bring restoration to those relationships.

He sees our sorrow, and sets us free

In stark contrast to the words and attitudes of early church fathers, thankfully the Bible is full of comfort and encouragement. The Daughters of Zion, it says, can rejoice greatly, because Jesus came to set the captives free and set at liberty those who were bound. (Luke 4:18).

Jesus was not bound either by the law or by the traditions of men. By his life, he showed women could be touched, talked to in public, included as disciples, treated as friends, and taught — even though Roman, Greek and Jewish tradition excluded women from all of the above.

Has History always excluded women?

For much of my adult life, I had lived under the widespread notion that the culture of learning and religion in the West had always excluded women. However, in my search for God's heart toward women, I happened to pick up the book *A World without Women* by David F. Noble. Noble's premise, which he supports with scholarly research: The male-dominated world of science and learning in the West is *not* the product of a world that has *always* excluded women. He demonstrates that the history of the church, the world's center of learning throughout most of its first millennium, records a *gradual* move toward the exclusion of women.

According to Noble, during the first thousand years of Christianity the situation for women was vastly different. As the church moved toward a celibate clergy by the 12th century, however, the gap between the clergy and the laity widened. This accompanied the late medieval move toward male dominance over the practices and institutions of higher learning

By reconstructing the history of the early church through the first millennium, he was able to demonstrate a very different world for women in the era that began with the inclusion of women in the earthly ministry of Jesus Christ. He discusses the way the apostle Paul honors various women leaders in the church and his rejection of celibacy as an ideal for the church. Paul, he says, " ... upheld the centrality of marriage and relied upon the authority and resources of the household to spread the gospel (which resulted in) a household church and a married church leadership" (page 6).

He also points out that the church in the house operated under a very different authority structure. Influence and leadership in the household fell largely to women. And those who were most influential in the household were often most influential in household churches. In addition, widows, especially from households of wealth, became primary benefactresses and influential voices in the early church.

Early evidence suggests a strong movement to elevate virginity and sexual purity as the absolute ideal for Christian life. In Nicaea, in the year 325, the First Ecumenical Council of the church rejected a call for clerical celibacy by the Spanish bishops and "defended marriage as an "honorable state' for clergy as well as laity" (page 7).

Eastern Christianity never did fully embrace the notion of a celibate clergy. In the West marriage among clergy remained the norm through most of the first millennium, in spite of serious challenges. Opportunities for women in the era of married clergy and a church centered around the household remained. But as the church became a separate institution and celibacy became the norm, males came more and more to monopolize clerical positions.

Beginning in the 4th century, however, monastic life provided a notable exception. Monasteries rose as opportunities for men and women to fully enter into religious life by turning their backs on the world, including material wealth and human sexuality.

In the case of Monasticism, women who embraced celibacy were often elevated to positions of leadership in monasteries and abbeys, which were the center of religious life. Historical evidence from as late as the ninth century attests to female abbesses and prioresses presiding over double monasteries where both men and women lived.

Jesus told the women, "Weep for yourselves!"

On his way to the cross, when virtually all of his male followers had abandoned him, Jesus spoke with great compassion to the women who remained with him and wept for him.

> *Jesus turned and said to them, "Daughters of Jerusalem, do not weep for me; weep for yourselves and for your children. For the time will come when you will say, 'Blessed are the barren women, the wombs that never bore and the breasts that never nursed!' Then they will say to the mountains, 'Fall on us!' and to the hills, 'Cover us!' For if men do these things when the tree is green, what will happen when it is dry?" (Luke 23:28-31).*

Did Jesus look ahead to the day when women would be falsely excluded from ministry and servant leadership in the church because of the traditions of men?

In the monastic life of the church women were offered a certain level of equality with their brothers. Until at least the ninth century after Jesus' death women who gave up their right to marry and bear children could dwell in monasteries and participate fully in the administration of the church (Noble, 3-39). Of course, as the first millennium of church history gave way to the second, these short-lived privileges for women came to an end.

For a season, however, the women who wept for Jesus might indeed have looked ahead and envied their celibate sisters who had never born children. At least for a season these barren women had achieved a small measure of the promise made centuries before. How tragic would it be to have received your redemption and to have been set at liberty by the Son of God, only to have your liberty taken away by men who could not handle the change God had intended to bring?

Redemption changed our relationship to God

> *But now in Christ Jesus you who once were far away have been brought near through the blood of Christ. For he himself is our peace, who has made the two one and has destroyed the barrier, the dividing wall of hostility, by abolishing in his flesh the law with its commandments and regulations. His purpose was to create in himself one new man out of the two, thus making peace, and in this one body to reconcile both of them to God through the cross, by which he put to death their hostility. He came and preached peace to you who were far away and peace to those who were near* (Eph. 2:13-17).

While this passage is generally accepted as a welcome to Gentiles who have been brought into the kingdom of God along side Jewish believers, it may well include other formerly disenfranchised people. Just as Galatians 3:28 brings down the dividing wall between Jew and Gentile, slave and free, and male and female, it seems not a great stretch to read this passage as a confirmation that those once far away and excluded are brought near because of Jesus. Where once there was barrier and dividing wall, now there is peace.

How comforting for a woman, for me, to read this passage as if it speaks about her, about me. Before Christ came, women were virtually excluded from the religious life of Israel. After Christ came, as we have seen, women enjoyed a period of relative freedom and inclusion in the life and ministry of the church. During all this time, however, men of influence tried to impose their own prejudice against women onto the practices and traditions of the church.

Ephesians 2 reinforces God's intent for all those who had been kept far away from fully participating in worship, study and the knowledge of God.

Now she who was *once far away* has *been brought near through the blood of Christ*. In redemption God has again *made the two* (male and female, in addition to Jew and Gentile) *one*, the way he intended in creation.

The dividing wall of hostility erected between men and women after the fall has been *destroyed*, along with all of the laws and regulations that kept women from enjoying full and equal participation in life and faith.

God's purpose has always been to *"create in himself one new man* (one person, one flesh) *out of the two ... And in this one body to reconcile both of them to God through the cross."*

By the cross (redemption) he *"put to death their hostility. He came and preached peace to you who were far away,"* sisters, *"... and peace to those who were near."*

It is liberating to notice the parallels between the language used to describe the relationship of men and women in marriage (the two shall become one) and the language used to describe the reconciliation that comes between people (God made the two one). I do not believe the parallel is accidental.

God fully intended, and Paul is the writer who makes it clear, to break down the barriers that once separated some people from God and from one another. He tore the curtain from top to bottom. He brought near those who were once far off. He destroyed the barrier and put to death our hostility. He made us all one in Christ Jesus.

I stated before that I think Paul may get falsely accused of disagreeing with his own words when it comes to women in ministry. We should remind ourselves of the times when Paul recognizes the ministry of women in his writings. In Romans 16:1, he says, *"I commend unto you Phoebe our sister, which is a servant (deacon) of the church which is at Cenchrea."* In verse 3 he greets *"Priscilla and Aquila, my helpers (fellow laborers) in Christ Jesus."* In verse 7, he salutes *"Junia, ... of note among the apostles."* In Galatians 3, it is Paul who writes: *"There is neither Jew nor Greek, there is neither bond nor free, there is neither male nor female: for ye are all **one** in Christ Jesus (3:28).*

If God intended the barriers between men and women to come down through the redemption of Jesus Christ, then we should not be found stubbornly resisting him because of our tradition. If God intends for men and women to be **one** (Galatians 3:28) in his body, the church, it should be worth our time to look again at our traditions (the things we have always believed and done about men and women in the church). We also may need to look again at our traditional interpretation of some scriptures, especially some words of Paul, to see if they line up with the rest of the word. We do not want to be found *"Making the word of God of no effect through your tradition which you have handed down,"* (Mark 7:13.)

God's heart in Galatians

Probably the book in the Bible that best speaks to me about God's heart toward women is Galatians. Here Paul labors to help us understand the freedom that came to us in Jesus Christ. We have said that once, among God's people, a Father's inheritance always went to the first-born son. Jesus has been called the first born among the brethren. Because of his wonderful love, those of us who believe have been called, "joint heirs," and "heirs according to the promise," (Gal. 3:29) which is very good news for women and younger sons.

When Paul wrote Galatians, even members of the original twelve were falling back on old ways to gain God's approval. They could not pull themselves away from the sign of the old covenant, circumcision. The sign was for Jews. It was for sons. In fact, before Christ came, most religious participation and privilege was reserved for Jewish males.

He told them, "You are all sons of God through faith in Christ Jesus, for all of you who were baptized into Christ have clothed yourselves with Christ" (26-27).

I believe Paul knew that some of us would hear his words and still try to disqualify ourselves from coming into our full inheritance as sons of God. Any woman, slave or Greek in Paul's hearing might have felt left out of the full inheritance of the saints because he or she was not part of the right group. But Paul answered all of their fears and objections with verse 28: *"There is neither Jew nor Greek, slave nor free, male nor female, for you are all one in Christ Jesus."*

Don't take this wrong, but I believe God showed me something else about this passage. When Paul said I am a son because I have clothed myself with Christ, he did not say I have clothed myself with Christ's *clothing*.

I have put on Christ. I am clothed with *him*. Just in case anyone might have trouble recognizing this woman (or this slave or this Greek) as a son of God, God has given me a new identity. **I look just like he does.**

In my spirit I can almost hear Paul say, "Is Christ divided? Did he have to provide one salvation for Greeks and slaves and women, and another for freeborn Jewish males? Oh you foolish Galatians!"

He continues his instruction by talking about the day when the heir was still a child, an illustration pregnant with meaning for every son of God. For while we were yet children under the law, we found ourselves subject to guardians and trustees. It didn't matter that we owned the whole estate. Being children required us to be in submission to our father's servants (4:1-3). But as we grew in favor and in knowledge, as we left our childhood behind, we knew our father had appointed a day when we could come into our full inheritance.

Choosing my full inheritance

Have you ever thought about the perpetual childhood of women in the church? Can a woman who is forever subject to the guardianship of her Father's servants, ever truly come into her full inheritance?

This too I asked my loving Father. This time I almost heard an audible voice. "That's up to you."

"What!?" I felt my passion rising again. But gently the Spirit of God began to show me. When I first became a believer, I was like a newborn, needing *"the sincere milk of the word,"* (1 Peter 2:22) and needing others to guide me and teach me in the way I should go. There comes a time, though, when I need to put away childish things (1 Cor. 13:11). There comes a time when I must know, without a trace of doubt, that **I too have every right to come into my full inheritance as a son of God.**

> *"But when the time had fully come, God sent his Son, born of a woman, born under law, to redeem those under law, that we might receive the full rights of sons" (Gal. 4:4,5).*

Just like grace, my inheritance is mine when I comprehend it and choose to embrace it. With grace I can choose to put myself back under the law and make the grace of God of no effect. If I choose to live under the law or under the guardianship of the law's advocates, I voluntarily give up my right to grace, or my right to live as a son of God with the full rights of sonship.

My faith is a choice, and without it I cannot please God. Living under grace is a choice, and if I choose instead to live under the security of the law, I have fallen from grace. And living in the full right of sonship is also a choice.

As a woman, I can choose to remain under the guardianship of the Father's servants, or I can choose to believe God has clothed me with Christ and made me a son of God. I can believe the time has fully come, that God sent his Son, born of a woman (like me) to redeem me completely and give me the full rights of a son.

This is not about rebellion. And it's not about my acting or dressing like a man. This is about my faith in the complete redemption of Jesus Christ. Such faith means I will bring my new identity in Christ with me as I live and work, and as I attempt to understand the Scriptures. I will be walking in the full rights of a son of God when I attempt to understand the words attributed to Paul that sound as if my redemption as a woman is less complete.

I can choose to see myself as a daughter of Eve, bride of the first Adam, forever bearing the guilt of her sin. Or I can see myself as fully redeemed. I can see myself as the bride of the second Adam, Jesus Christ, redeemed by his grace to become the righteousness of God in him.

The second choice takes courage. It means I have to take God at his Word. It means I will walk in newness of life, not bound by the "basic principles of the world," even when those principles have crept into the church.

It means I shall not be pusillanimous (*faint hearted, lily-livered, cowardly*). I will have to courageously, as woman, bear my part of the image of God. I will praise him, for I am fearfully and wonderfully made, made as a woman, made in the image of God, and growing from glory to glory into the image of his dear Son.

Women, how would you like to declare: "I have been made into a son of God (while remaining fully female). I am an heir of the promises. I am grown, and I am no longer in need of a guardian. I now have the full rights of a son of God. Once I was outside, now I have been allowed to come in close. All things are lawful to me, but I will not come under the power of any."

Would it be rebellion? Or would it be a faith declaration?

Would you like to declare it with me?

"I will believe the word of God is true and profitable for me, a woman saved by grace and set at liberty by the Son of God!"

Appendix 1: Advice to Pastors

In this appendix you will find, first a brief interview with my home church pastor, Howard Matthews, from HomeFront Church in Grandville Michigan. Second, you will find an article by Lola Scobey entitled "Crafting a Church without Walls." The article first appeared in the Fall, 2002 issue of *Mutuality,* a publication of Christians for Biblical Equality. (www.cbeinternational.org)

An Interview with Howard Matthews

Q. What have you and the leadership team done to promote or defend women in positions of leadership at HomeFront?

A. We have an advantage because we are a new church plant. We have been intentional and upfront about wanting women on our leadership team from the beginning. We also seek to make the participation of women in leadership visible to anyone who visits the church, browses our website or reads our literature.

Q. What results have you seen because of including women in leadership?

A. The women on the leadership team at HomeFront often demonstrate their unique qualities which make them indispensable to the ministry of this church. Whether it shows up in a meeting when one of the women calls us back to Christ-like compassion, or in the organization and planning required to launch a ministry, we depend on the women God has given us to be part of the team.

Q. How would you handle opposition or objections to women serving in leadership positions?

A.Because we have been upfront about including women from the start, I'm sure people with serious objections have not chosen to be a part of HomeFront. When new people come, I don't think it takes them long to figure out our stand on men and women in ministry. Ministry leader names, including the women, are listed on our website, and they are referred to during our announcement time. We try to be intentional in making women a regular part of our services.

Q. How do your Sunday messages reinforce the idea of both men and women in ministry?

A. I have not done any specific teaching about the women's issue from the podium, but every time I teach, I am careful to use language that does not exclude women. If the Bible passage I'm reading was meant to speak to everyone present, I choose a translation that includes everyone. I often use *The Message*, and sometimes the TNIV (*Today's New International Version*). I was encouraged when leaders of Willow Creek Church came out in support of the TNIV as a more accurate translation regarding gender.

Q. Is there anything else you want to do?

A. I think we may want to add a value statement about women in ministry to our church's statement of values. We regularly review one or more of our values during a Sunday message. And of course the values are posted on our website (homefrontchurch.org).
Sometimes it (dealing with the women's issue) can be like walking a tightrope. People who disagree look at certain verses in the Bible. But when the Bible was written, society was very patriarchal. Sometimes the ideas were not so much God's desire as they were simply the way things were.

Three more pastors weigh in

The following is an article which appeared in the Fall 2002 issue of *Mutuality,* a publication of Christians for Biblical Equality. (www.cbeinternational.org)

Crafting a Church Without Walls

Three Pastors Share How Their Churches Embraced Gender Equality, and What They Learned Along the Way

by Lola Scobey

Whether it's a church with about 85 members, one with 850 members, or one with around 8,000 members, three gift-based churches, as described by their pastors, practice a model of church life that is not typical, regardless of size.

These three pastors — Austin Stouffer, Jo Ann Kunz and John Ortberg — have steadily guided their members to use their spiritual gifts in an environment of gender equality. And each states that their gift-based church acquired its egalitarian stance from one fundamental: studying the Scriptures with other Christians.

Austin Stouffer is pastor of Grace Evangelical Free Church in Thunder Bay, Ontario, a small but vibrant church of 75-90 members, with the written mandate: "to reach all walks of life in a class-free, self-help oriented, biblically stimulating environment, while still remaining within our denomination."

Stouffer, the son of a mother who preached, worked 10 years in social work with abused women and broken families before entering seminary. There he encountered what he terms "extreme hierarchical views" on gender. However, earning a master's degree and then a doctorate in divinity gave him a grasp of New Testament Greek and Hebrew that reinforced his innate sense of gender equality.

Six years ago, Stouffer, a marriage and family therapist as well as pastor, was asked by five mostly young, middle-class couples to lead them in starting a new church. "I explained eight 'musts' that I would insist on if I pastored another church," he says. "One of them was absolute gender equality."

The group then asked him to present a mini-workshop in gender and giftedness. "To my surprise," Stouffer says, "they were delighted with my explanations."

Today Stouffer says, "Grace Evangelical has unalterably entrenched the following statement in their own church Constitution: Members of both genders ... may serve in any capacity or hold any office in the church."

This includes serving on the Pastoral Care Council, which functions basically like an elder board. In addition, Stouffer says that when he goes on holidays, the committee that chooses lay people to take the pulpit "usually chooses women over men two to one, based on ability to preach."

Bible Study Prompts Church Change

Jo Ann Kunz began attending Hosanna Christian Fellowship in Lititz, Penn., in 1980, only a few months after meeting Christ as an adult. Hosanna is the only church she has ever been a member of — and today she is senior pastor.

As a new member, it soon became obvious Kunz was gifted to teach and had a strong leadership gift. But recognizing these gifts in an environment that only affirmed them in men led to confusion for Kunz. She describes her mixed emotions as "thinking that this really must be something God was doing — but also fearing that something was wrong with it, wrong with me."

She had to know the truth, not just for herself, but for every other gifted woman she saw in her church. As a result, she and her male pastor studied the Scriptures together in his office for 4-8 hours a day, 3—4 days a week.

"We began by putting aside everything we had been taught and just approached the Scriptures with as unbiased a mind as we could," she says. "When we really saw what Genesis 1-3 was saying — that woman is the mirror image of man, equal in every way, I put my head down on the desk and wept. What freedom!"

These studies led the male pastor to preach numerous sermons on gender equality. Today Hosanna is the only church in an area Kunz describes as "very conservative and steeped in religious tradition" which has both a female senior pastor and a female associate pastor as well as a policy that "no door is closed because of gender."

Mega-Church Has Foundation of Equality

John Ortberg came to gigantic, national news-making Willow Creek Church as teaching pastor eight years ago. Holding a master's of divinity and a doctorate in clinical psychology, he was formerly senior pastor of a church in Los Angeles and is a recognized author in the areas of spiritual formation and leadership. Willow Creek is located in South Barrington, Ill., a suburb of Chicago, and often has as many as 17,000 people attend services.

Ortberg credits his church's gift-based ministries to Dr. Gilbert Bilezikian's legacy there. A noted Bible scholar whom Ortberg calls a "founding wisdom figure" of Willow Creek, Bilezikian led the initial leaders through a process of studying what the Bible says about a woman's place in the church and family. This laid a foundation for the church, which now includes women not only as elders and as teaching pastors (i.e. preachers), but in every aspect of church life.

Ortberg himself initiated a series at Willow Creek's mid-week service, typically attended by 6,000 people, called "What Does the Bible Say About Men and Women?" "This is an issue which goes un-addressed at too many churches," he says. "Our senior pastor had been speaking on leadership at a conference and received a note afterwards that said, 'Help, I'm a leader trapped in the body of a woman.' We need very direct teaching on these issues."

Building Blocks for Change

All three pastors report that simply studying the Scriptures with full openness allows the Holy Spirit to bring about change in church life.

But further discussion reveals a shared experience: Each has grown to see that while right knowledge can drive change, full-orbed wisdom is ultimately required to change a church. They describe a breed of wisdom that includes resolute courage, spiritual maturity, clear focus, careful planning, flexibility, perseverance, compassion and respect.

Stauffer acknowledges that it is easier to affirm gender equality in a church "from scratch," as both he and Willow Creek have done.

But wherever you start, Willow Creek's Ortberg points out, "As time passes, you have to recognize you will have a diverse congregation. And it can be deadly for leaders to assume that the congregation knows what the leaders believe."

Based on Willow Creek's experience, Ortberg recommends several steps:

1. Begin with leaders doing a careful Bible study.

2. Constantly cast vision that the church is organized around giftedness.

3. Do clear, careful, sound, exegetical teaching on this issue.

4. Offer or even require members to attend seminars that identify each person's spiritual gifts.

5. Find gifted people who can be models and let people experience gift-based ministry.

"When people experience a great leadership or teaching gift exercised by a woman, change happens," Ortberg says, recalling a man mentored by Nancy Beach, one of their two female teaching pastors. "This man told me, 'I've never done this before. I have unresolved emotions about it. But no one has ever developed me the way she has.'"

Even beyond such concrete steps, Ortberg suggests allowing a lot of time, being persistent, and realizing that change on this issue is a subcategory of how to bring about change in a church in general. "You've got to discern," he says, "how much change can this church take?"

All three pastors agree that change requires strong intentionality and that conflict is inevitable. "Don't just sit there hoping things will change," says Kunz. "And don't think change will come without opposition and conflict. Change by its very nature brings conflict. As Flannery O'Connor said, 'Healing only occurs when the waters are disturbed.'"

But Kunz is hopeful. "Remember," she says, "experts tell us it only takes 2 percent of a group to change the culture of a group. Only 2 percent. You may lose some folks. But you will gain far more."

Baby Steps in Stubborn Churches

How do leaders respond if members are resistant —and how do members respond if church leadership is resistant? Even today, Stouffer's denomination does not share his views on gender equality and still refuses to ordain women.

"Gender equality simply cannot be attained by one nuclear confrontation," Stouffer says, citing how even moderate efforts concerning gender are often interpreted as aggressive by others. "I've had a lot better success with small steps," he adds.

Stouffer highlights extensive New Testament Greek exegesis and word etymology as an effective small step. "No one has ever been offended when I have explained proper word usage," he says. He also uses a balance of men and women in sermon illustrations and coaches the church's nominating committee to always seek the most competent and qualified person for any position, regardless of gender.

Ortberg suggests networking with other churches that have gone through change. "It's key here to not lose hope," he says. "Because when you lose hope, you lose the motivation to act. Networking will help you keep going."

Kunz acknowledges that the pastor of her church did it the hard way. "The only congregational education was from the pulpit," she says. "There were a series of messages with little preparation for the congregation and these messages were quite 'in your face' — confrontational, combative, almost arrogant. The attitude of the messenger caused more resistance than there needed to be."

Ultimately, Ortberg advises leaders to return to the basics. "I try to keep the whole situation rooted in love," he says. "I try to teach rightly. I try to show appropriate pastoral sensitivity to people who disagree. I try to honor their understanding of Scripture, to remember that they are not bad people because they see it differently. I work to achieve community; that's a whole lot more important than proving myself right."

Discerning God's Direction

But despite the missteps implicit in a learning curve, all of these churches affirm gender equality today. What if change in one's own church seems very far away? How does a church member know whether to stay or to leave?

"If you see small battles bringing small victories, hang in there if you can," Stouffer counsels. "However, if staying requires you to renounce or compromise your fundamental beliefs in any area, you're not doing yourself or the congregation any favors by staying."

"Ultimately it's a discernment question," Orberg notes. "What is your concept of commitment? The Desert Fathers and Mothers said, 'Wherever you find yourself, don't easily leave.' This is how you grow. You've got to have a whole underlying sense of what commitment means to you. So, be very careful before you commit to a church in the first place."

Kunz, who is a spiritual director as well as pastor, also focuses on discernment. "First, you must get alone with God and discern direction directly from him," she says. "God is the only one who knows whether that church, that leader, will ever change. God is the only one who knows whether you will be part of changing that church or not. You've got to hear from God."

From Paralyzed in Pew to Active in ministry

How have these churches benefited from allowing every member to practice God-given gifts regardless of gender? "It's huge," says Ortberg. "Otherwise, we'd be working with one hand tied behind our back. We'd be literally impoverished."

Stouffer says the 30 years he has spent as a marriage and family therapist has led to his passion about biblical equality. "It is my impression that most churches are far more accepting of a divorced or separated husband than a wife in that position," says Stouffer. "At Grace, fully one-third of our adults are divorced, separated or remarried. In our group, they feel accepted and loved the way they are, and nurtured in the Word to become all they can be in Christ."

Kunz observes husbands and wives in her church experience what she calls "deeper and more intimate relationships when they drop all the cookie-cutter roles." Plus, "At Hosanna," she says, "half the gifts of the church are not sitting dormant because the women have been sidelined."

Furthermore, Kunz has seen a remarkable effect even outside her own church. "A few church leaders in the area have come to believe in gender equality — and a few more have come to at least tolerate it," she says, "because they can't question what God is doing in the midst of our church. In the first 18 months I was senior pastor, almost 100 people were saved. That's a God thing!"

~~~

Lola Scobey is co-founder of Audio-Therapy Innovations, an entrepreneurial company that for 17 years has pioneered the use of music therapy for children. She is also a writer, editor, marketing consultant and certified spiritual director.

Appendix II: Discussion Questions

Introduction – Is Exclusion God's Idea?

1) Reflecting on "inclusion" and "exclusion" as they relate to members of the church as the body of Christ:

a) In congregations you know, what kinds of restrictions are there against certain kinds of people or groups participating in church membership?

b) What kinds of restrictions apply to various types of ministry, like teaching, counseling, praying or reading Scripture, serving communion, or helps?

c) What are the criteria behind any restrictions you can name? (For example: education, referral or recommendations, doctrinal agreement, race, age, social class, marital status, maturity, gender, sexual orientation, etc.)

d) Consider whether you could apply the same type of criteria in your workplace, or in a public institution (If there is a difference between the public arena and your church policy, is it justified? Why or why not?

2) Can a woman fulfill her call to ministry vicariously through her husband? Why or Why not?

3) Think about your current set of beliefs. What is the biggest change you've seen between what you once believed and what you believe today?

4) How have your traditionally held beliefs or values (or those of your family) been challenged as you matured and/or new information became available?

5) If you were to change from a belief in the traditional idea of male leadership and authority in home and church to a belief in equality between men and women in those two areas, how do you think it would affect your life?

Chapter 1 — Who does she think she is?

1) If you have ever been accused or suspected of rebellion for disagreeing or for challenging a tradition or belief held by family, friends, or church, was it a fair charge? What did you do?

2) When it comes to studying and understanding the issues surrounding men and women in the church, do you think that either men or women are more motivated or qualified to find answers? What are the potential pitfalls for either men or women attempting to shed light on the gender issue in the church?

3) Names and labels for people can be emotionally charged. Discuss ways we label people or groups in order to express our disapproval or approval of them, for example in politics. In all the various flavors of Christianity, can you think of some names and labels that communicate bias?

4) How does this discussion apply to the label *traditionalist?*

5) How does it apply to the label *evangelical feminist?*

6) Take time to look closely at the two opposing viewpoints as expressed by CBMW and CBE found on pages 26-28. Which statement of belief comes closest to your current beliefs? Why?

7) Pretend for a moment that you are a member of the opposite group. How would you argue their position?

8) From each of the two possible positions, try to imagine the consequences if your position turns out to be wrong. I.E. if the traditional view is right, but people fail to follow it, or if the biblical feminists are right, but people fail to recognize it …

9) How might the issue of equality between men and women be related to the issues of race and class distinction?

Chapter 2   First Adam and First Eve

1) Retell your traditional version of the creation of the first man and the first woman, the way you remember it. Now look for ways your remembered version differs from the account in the first two chapters of Genesis.

2) Do you think men and women express God's image differently? If so, how?

3) Reflect on the statement, "Together, Adam and Eve were more like God than Adam had been alone." In what ways might this be true?

a)   What limitations did Adam alone face in order to be like God?

b)   What limitations did Eve alone face in order to be like God?

c)   This chapter implies that married couples and individuals living in community are more like God, or more able to represent God to the world, than individuals who are isolated from the rest of God's people. Do you think this is so? Why or why not?

4) In Scriptures we often encounter masculine words when the correct meaning includes both male and female. For example in Ephesians 2:15, it states Christ's purpose "to create one new man out of the two..." How do you sort these meanings out when you read the Bible?

5) What assumptions are often made regarding rank or importance based on the order in which God created male and female? Does the order of creation imply rank in any other instance?

6) Before reading this chapter, how would you assume Adam and Eve divided their work in the Garden? Who was given dominion?

7) What is your impression about the meaning of the word help-meet? Does this meaning fit when the term "help-meet" is used to describe God's relationship to us? (As in, "God is a helper fit for us.")

Chapter 3   Fallen Adam and Fallen Eve

1) Can you think of ways women are or have been encouraged to behave more like children than adults?

a) Do you think it's possible to be both feminine and adult? Give examples to support your answer.

b) If a woman is strong, independent, logical and decisive, might she appear too masculine? If so, what is the alternative? Is your answer as true for adolescent girls and young women as it is for older women?

c)   What subtle differences in meaning might arise depending on whether the following verse is read by a male believer or a female believer? *For God hath not given us the spirit of fear; but of power, and of love, and of a sound mind. 2 Timothy 1:7*   N o t e : in a group, ask at least one male and one female to give a personal response to this verse.

2) Retell the story of the temptation and fall of Adam and Eve as you remember it. Compared to the account in Genesis 3, does your remembered account differ in details or tone?

a)   What reason would your remembered account give for the serpent first approaching Eve with temptation?

b)   What does your remembered account suggest as Adam's motivation for taking the fruit offered by Eve?

c)   Did you remember God's punishment including a curse on Adam and Eve? How does the idea that God cursed only the ground and the serpent effect your understanding?

d)   Had you seen the subordination of Eve to Adam as beginning with Creation? How might your sense of male/female relationships change with the idea it came only after the Fall?

3) On an emotional level, whom do you hold more responsible for introducing sin into God's perfect creation and bringing about what we call the Fall?

a) If Adam, why?

b) If Eve, why?

4) Genesis 3:16 describes the situation between a man and a woman after the Fall, ("thy desire shall be to thy husband, and he shall rule over thee."). If you can, give other examples where Scriptures merely describe how things are without making a law.

Chapter 4 The Maker of Adam and Eve

1) Think about your own image of God. Do you tend to picture God as a male figure? Is it difficult to visualize anything but a male when you think of God? Why or why not?

2) The Bible uses feminine imagery to teach us about God. Give any examples you can remember. Here are a few references to get you started: Isaiah 49:13-15, 66: 13; Isaiah 42:14; Psalms 123: 2.

3) How does knowing God as Father help us know God?

4) How might we be helped in knowing God by focusing on the feminine images provided in the Scripture? What might we miss about God's nature by focusing only on the masculine imagery in the Scripture? For example:
   a)   The hen gathering her chicks-Matt 23:37;
   b)   The mother eagle-Duet. 32:11-12;
   c)   The nurturer- Isaiah. 49:13-15.

5) Think about your own relationship to both your mother and your father. In what ways might you benefit from knowing God as a mother in addition to knowing God as a father?

Chapter 5   Daughters of Eve in the Old Testament

1) Read 2 Kings 22:8-23:3. While many names are mentioned, who were the main characters of the story? Had you heard of any of these characters before reading this passage?

2) Look at and compare the following images of God found in the New Testament. Try to notice how familiar the images are, and how often you have heard them used to teach what God is like.

a) God is like a good shepherd who leaves his 99 sheep to go off and search for the one that is lost.

b) God is like the housecleaning wife who scours her floor looking for the coin that is lost.

Can you think of any reasons we might hear more often about God the good shepherd? Do you, for instance, personally know more shepherds, or do you know more housecleaning wives?

3) If churches and Sunday Schools selectively teach us about male images for God and frequently leave out the feminine images and stories, how will our ability to know God be affected?

a) What might some of the reasons for such selectivity be?

b) What should we do about it?

4) Would the 1950's American family model fit your family's current lifestyle? Why or why not? Do you wish it would, or think it should? Why?

5) Some have said biblical examples of women in leadership are the exception to God's rule. If God does not like women in leadership, what would make him violate his own will or his own rule?

a) Note: If your answer is, men are sometimes unavailable, timid, or disobedient, how does that compare to God using a donkey to prophesy or declaring even the rocks and hills will praise his name?

b) Name some occasions when God used a reluctant or unlikely male to do his bidding?

6) In some third world countries, women are not allowed to show themselves or speak to men in public. Many suffer physical abuse by angry husbands and fathers. If Jesus walked the earth today, what do you think he would do for these women?

Chapter 6   Daughters of Eve in the New Testament

1) From what you know of New Testament Scriptures, what would God think about excluding people of certain races or social classes from full participation in the church?

a) Is there anything to prevent a born-again Jew or a former slave or a poor person from rising to the level of pastor, elder, or deacon in the church?

b) Reading Galatians 3:28, (*neither Jew nor Greek, bond nor free, male nor female*): can we also include women in the above list? Why or why not?

2) Read Galatians 3:28 again. Logically we know all distinction between races, classes, and genders did not end when we were redeemed by Christ's blood. Discuss the extent of the changes this verse suggests, making us all one in Christ Jesus.

3) Jesus entered the scene during a period of Greco-Roman history when women had few legal rights and freedoms. The cultural life of the Jews also held women under strict patriarchal rules. Recall some of the ways Jesus defied the patriarchal culture of the day and treated women differently.

4) Jesus often taught using stories, by-passing the letter of the law to reach for a deeper truth. Recall stories Jesus told about women.

5) Among Jesus' closest friends were Mary and Martha of Bethany. Recall teachings you have heard about Mary and Martha, especially Martha's complaint of Mary's failure to help with the women's work.

a) How have your teachers extracted the meaning or the moral of the story?

b) Have you ever heard anyone suggest that Mary had taken the demeanor of a good student, sitting at the feet of the Rabbi?

6) Have you ever heard of Junia? (Romans 16:7) Scholars agree this is a feminine name. Paul says to salute her, and Andronicus, his kinsmen and fellow prisoners. What else does Paul say about them? What do you think they did to earn this description?

Chapter 7   But the Scriptures Plainly Say

1) How does the suggestion of finding alternative interpretations of certain scriptures make you feel?

2) If you need to find out what a passage of Scripture really means, what do you do?

3) If a passage of Scripture is addressed to a particular person or a particular group of people, is the message always for all people and for all time? Look at the following passages, then find some examples of your own to discuss.

a) 1Timothy 5:23 (*Drink no longer water, but use a little wine for thy stomach's sake and thine often infirmities.*)

b) Philemon 1:22 NIV (*And one thing more: Prepare a guest room for me, because I hope to be restored to you in answer to your prayers.*)

c) 2 Timothy 4:13, 21. (*When you come, bring the cloak that I left with Carpus at Troas, and my scrolls, especially the parchments. ... Do your best to get here before winter.*)

4) Bible translators have often chosen to use masculine nouns or pronouns, even when the original Greek did not specify masculine or feminine. Has the choice of the translators affected your understanding of the text with regard to male and female issues?

5) Answer Question 4 in light of the following examples:

a) Phil. 1:27 "*... stand firm in one spirit, contending as one man for the faith of the gospel.*" The original says to stand firm in one spirit as with one soul, and does not use the word *man*.

b) Heb. 2:11 "*Both the one who makes men holy and those who are made holy are of the same family. So Jesus is not ashamed to call them brothers.*" The original speaks of God who sanctifies and those who are sanctified. It does not use the word *man*.

Note: The word *brothers*, though sometimes used to denote male siblings, is often used to refer to men and women who shared a common belief in Christ. Example: Acts 1:14-16

c) 1Tim. 3:1 "*This is a true saying, If a man desire the office of a bishop, he desireth a good work*" (KJV). To their credit, other than the King James, most English translations do not change the original word meaning "*anyone*" to "*a man.*"

d) If you could read these passages without any masculine words supplied by the translator, would it affect your understanding of the text?

6) In what ways have you observed Christians using propaganda to make their case, for example, by name calling or oversimplifying the opponent's point of view?

7) Here is a partial list of things that could be included in a set of New Testament Laws, some of them based on a literal interpretation of New Testament text, and some pulled forward from the Old Testament. The list is just to give you something to think about, and is in no way intended to state which things we should obey and which things we are free to ignore. Discuss the impact of these passages if Christians are truly under a covenant of grace and not of law:

a) Malachi 3:10 - *Bring ye all the tithes into the storehouse.*

b) Exodus 20:9-10 - *Remember the Sabbath day, to keep it holy. Six days shalt thou labour, and do all thy work ...*

c) Matt. 5:29-30 - *If your right eye causes you to sin, gouge it out and throw it away ... And if your right hand causes you to sin, cut it off and throw it away.* (NIV)

d) I Tim. 2:12 - *I do not permit a woman to teach or to have authority over a man; she must be silent.* (NIV)

e) 1Cor. 14:34-35 - *Women should remain silent in the churches. They are not allowed to speak, but must be in submission, as the Law says. If they want to inquire about something, they should ask their own husbands at home; for it is disgraceful for a woman to speak in the church.* (NIV)

f) 1Tim. 2:9 - *... also that women should adorn themselves modestly and sensibly in seemly apparel, not with braided hair or gold or pearls or costly attire.* (RSV)

Chapter 8 "As Christ is the Head of the Church"

1) Many words in our language have both a literal and a figurative meaning. The literal meaning may remain constant, while the figurative changes over time. Grass and weed may describe the stuff of our landscapes, but are interchangeable with words for pot or marijuana. A mouse is a literal creature we don't want in our house, but put it next to a computer and it's something else. Each generation has its own slang, its own metaphors, so that our language is always changing.

a)   Think of some more examples of words that mean something different today than they meant a decade or more ago.

b)   Think of some examples of words in the bible, especially in older translations like the King James, whose meaning has changed. Example: What does the King James call a donkey?

2) If you knew ahead of time, beyond all doubt, God made men and women fully equal, and both men and women are needed to fully reflect the image of God, and the redemption of Jesus Christ completely removed any restrictions on the roles of men and women in the home and the church, how would that knowledge effect your interpretation of passages typically cited by those who believe more traditionally?

3) How would you approach I Corinthians 11:3-16?

a)   Can you find any hints or evidence that the author (Paul) might have been addressing a specific group of people for a specific purpose?

b)   Are there words you can identify that might mean something different to us today than they would have meant when the letter was written?

c)   What parts of this passage, if any, sound like they might be more universal, or meant to apply to people outside the church of Corinth in the first or second century (for all people at all time)?

4) Look for some of the better examples of New Testament Scriptures that are clearly meant for all people for all time. List a few. To get you started, what did Jesus say when he was asked to identify the greatest of the commandments? (Matthew 22:36-40).

5) In both ancient and modern times, some honors and responsibilities have been conferred on the first-born child. What are some of these?

a)   A first-born child may be occasionally put in charge of his younger siblings, but it will almost always be for a limited time and in a limited way. What would it take for a first-born child to be given full responsibility and authority over the brothers and sisters who were born later?

b)   If this rare situation did exist, would it be permanent?

Chapter 9   "Let your women keep silent"

1) Read I Corinthians 14:33-35. Assume for a moment it means literally what it says, and it is a directive straight from heaven. How many people or churches do you know who follow it to the letter? Do you? If you are a woman, when was the last time you made any kind of noise in church, joyful or otherwise?

2) If we live under grace and not under law, how do we interpret "as says the law" in the passage?

3) In the practice of Christian religion, not uncommonly we find ourselves under some form of New Testament law, whether legitimate or not. Think about your own church and/or your own set of beliefs and religious practices. If you made a list of expectations, and then assigned each item on your list to a category of law or grace, how would you come out?

4) Consider the two possible solutions offered in this chapter to explain the apparent inconsistency of the passage with the rest of Paul's message. What do you think of the possibility that the lack of punctuation—like quotation marks—keeps modern readers from recognizing Paul is here restating the position he is attempting to correct?

5) What do you think of the idea that this passage was once a marginal note that eventually got copied into the text, though it had not been part of the text originally?

Chapter 10 "I Suffer Not a Woman"

1) What if the translators had chosen the words "Let your women learn in peace" instead of "in silence"? How might your first impression of Paul's meaning have been different?

2) Look at the following words, and discuss which ones seem to apply more to men than women or visa-versa, and why?
   a. Gentle, Quiet, Silent, Peaceful, Meek, Loving, Patient ...
   b. Authoritative, Dominant, Powerful, Of a Sound Mind ...

3) Read Matthew 20:25-27. What did Jesus say about those in authority?

4) Read 2 Timothy 1:7. What does God say about power, love, and a sound mind?

5) Galatians 5:22-23 gives us a list of the fruits of the Holy Spirit. Are any of these gender specific? Compare your answer to your response to question 2) a.

6) Besides learning in quiet peace, she was to learn in all submission. How does the word submission apply to men as well as women?

7) To usurp authority speaks of the misuse of authority. Look again at Matthew 20:25-27. How might a Christian misuse his or her authority?

8) Learning is always a prerequisite for someone who wants to teach. If the women in Ephesus were participating in the spreading of heresy, something had to change. What was Paul's prescription to Timothy to help bring about the change?

9) Think about church leaders you have known. Are you fortunate enough to know any who have exhibited the kind of humble servant leadership Christ taught and demonstrated in Matthew 20? Have you also seen abuse of authority by those who would "lord it over" their congregation? Compare the two types of leadership. Was gender a factor in either case?

10) Luke's account of Jesus' instruction about authority says when the kings of the Gentiles exercise lordship, they are called "benefactors," which implies one who rules his subjects for their own good (Luke 22:25-27). Yet, Jesus holds leaders in his kingdom to a much higher standard. How is "exercising lordship as a benefactor" different than the standard of leadership commanded by Christ?

11) Now compare that to the standard for husbands set in Eph. 5:25: *"Husbands, love your wives, as Christ loved the church and gave himself up for her."*

12) In the light of Eph. 5:25 and Luke 22:25-27, do you think Paul or Jesus intended a husband to exercise control (lordship) over his wife? Can a husband rule over his wife for her own good? Can his leadership be compared to that of a parent and child? Read Galatians 4:1-7. Who are the heirs of God? The heirs go from being children who are subject to the father's servants to walking in their full inheritance as sons. Does this apply only to males? Why or Why Not?

Chapter 11   Second Adam and Second Eve

1) Recall the story of Jesus' "Triumphal Entry" into Jerusalem. What images tell the story for you? (Matt. 21:5, John 12:15). Read Zechariah 9:9, and reflect on the word "daughter." Name as many feminine images as you can that relate to this story.

2) Why do you think Zechariah 9:9 specifically calls the daughters to rejoice?

3) Look again at he poem, *The Second Eve*, in this chapter. Reconstruct the events that brought about the birth of a bride, first for Adam, and then for Jesus, who is called the Second Adam.

4) Look again at Romans 5:6-11. Try the exercise suggested in the chapter, inserting the word *women* after the word *we*. If that causes you any discomfort, could you read it comfortably by inserting the word *men* instead, as Bible translators often did? What if you were to insert your own name, as Bible teachers often suggest, in order to make a Bible promise more personal?

5) In the marriage metaphor describing Christ and his church, Christ bears the masculine image of husband while we, the church or the bride of Christ, bear the feminine image. How might this affect, first, our role as members of the body of Christ, and second, our understanding of the role of men and women in families and the church?

   a.   Describe the role of the bride or wife according to the traditional ideal, and draw parallels to the role of men and women as members of Christ's church.

b.   Describe the role of the bride or wife in a model of equality. Draw parallels between this description and the role of men and women in the church.

Chapter 12   Eve Redeemed

1) If the church moved gradually from the inclusion of women in leadership roles to the nearly universal exclusion of women sometime after the first millennium, what does that suggest about God's intent for the role of women?

2) What evidence can you think of which will either support or refute the idea that women were gradually excluded from church leadership (in contrast to always excluded)?

3) If women who chose to live a celibate life and never bear children were given the freedom to live a meaningful life of quiet devotion and dedication to God and the church, can you imagine women today feeling envy toward them? What about during other periods of history?

4) Paul says, "You who were once far away have been brought near." Who might he be talking about? Read Ephesians 2:13-17 and Galatians 3:28 side by side.

5) Can all believers receive the full right of sons (Galatians 4:4-5)? What might that look like?

Works Cited

Belleville, Linda L. *Women Leaders and the Church, Three Crucial Questions*. Grand Rapids, MI: Baker, 2000.

Bilezikian, Gilbert. *Community 101, Reclaiming the Local Church as Community of Oneness*. Grand Rapids, MI: Zondervan, 1997.

Chittister, Joan. *In Search of Belief.* Liguori, MO: Liguori/Triumph, 1999.

Fee, Gordon D. *The First Epistle to the Corinthians: The New International Commentary on the New Testament.* Grand Rapids, MI: Wm B. Eerdmans, 1987. And *New International Biblical Commentary, 1 and 2 Timothy, Titus.* Peabody MA: Hendrickson Publishers, 1995.

Groothuis, Rebecca Merril. *Women Caught in the Conflict.* Grand Rapids, MI: Baker, 1994.

Hayter, Mary. *The New Eve in Christ.* Grand Rapids, MI: Wm B. Eerdmans, 1987.

Kroeger, Catherine Clark and Richard C. Kroeger. *I Suffer Not A Woman; Rethinking 1 Timothy 2:11-15 in Light of Ancient Evidence.* Grand Rapids, MI: Baker, 1992.

Noble, David F. *A World Without Women, The Christian Clerical Culture of Western Science.* Oxford and New York: Oxford University Press, 1992.

Rienstra, Marchiene Vroon. *Swallow's Nest, a Feminine Reading of the Psalms.* Grand Rapids, MI: Wm. B. Eerdmans, 2003.

Spencer, Aida Basancon with William David Spencer. *Beyond the Curse: Women Called to Ministry.* Peabody MA: Hendrickson Publishers, 1985.

Stott, John R.W. *Basic Christianity.* Downers Grove, IL: Inter-Varsity, 1958.

Strong's Dictionary and Concordance. Verse Search, Bible Research Systems 6.3, 1999.

Wolf, Fred Alan. *Taking the Quantum Leap, The New Physics for Nonscientists.* New York: Harper & Row, 1989.

Other Sources

Grenz, Stanley J. with Denise Muir Kjesbo. Women in the Church, A Biblical Theology of Women in Ministry. *Downers Grove, IL: Inter-Varsity, 1995.*

Groothuis, Rebecca Merrill. *Good News for Women, A Biblical Picture of Gender Equality.* Grand Rapids, MI: Baker, 1997.

Piper, John and Wayne Grudem, Ed. *Recovering Biblical Manhood & Womanhood, A Response to Evangelical Feminism.* Wheaton, IL: Crossway, 1991. (In defense of a subordinate role for women.)

Useful Web Sites

(www.)   juniapublishing.com
cbeinternational.org
equalitycentral.com
tniv.com

*   *   *   *   *   *   *

To order this book:

Order on-line   www.juniapublishing.com

Prices and Details:

Quantity		Price, each	Shipping
1	retail	$12.95	$2.00
2-4	save 20%	$10.36	$4.00
5-99	save 40%	$ 7.77	to be calculated

(50% discount for quantities of 100 or more)
Michigan residents add 06% sales tax

———— copy order blank or include the following information: ————

Mail orders to: Junia Publishing
PO Box 381
Jenison, MI 49429 0381

Quantity:_____X Price : $_____+ Shp $_____

Total enclosed (check or money order) $_____
Made payable to Junia Publishing
(credit card payments available through Paypal on the website)

Ship books to:

Name: _____

Address: _____

City State, Zip _____

e-mail and/or phone _____